Buck Up, Little Buckaroo

Buck Up, Little Buckaroo

MARY ELLEN EDMUNDS

DESERET
BOOK

Salt Lake City, Utah

Library of Congress Cataloging-in-Publication Data
Edmunds, Mary Ellen, author.
  Buck up, little buckaroo / Mary Ellen Edmunds.
      p. cm.
  Includes bibliographical references.
  ISBN 978-1-60641-949-6 (paperbound)
  1. Loneliness—Religious aspects—The Church of Jesus Christ of Latter-day Saints.
2. Mormons—Conduct of life.   I. Title.
  BV4911.E36 2011
  248.8'6—dc22   2011001630

Printed in the United States of America
Worzalla Publishing Co., Stevens Point, WI

10   9   8   7   6   5   4   3   2   1

To all who are kind and good, who help to make the world better
and the people who live in it less lonely.

"No man or woman can be strong, gentle, pure, and good,
without the world being better for it and without someone being helped and
comforted by the very existence of that goodness."
(Phillips Brooks)

Contents

Preface

It's been a challenge to write a book about loneliness. I didn't want to write one that would make someone who was lonely feel lonelier, or that would cause someone who seldom if ever feels lonely to say, "This isn't my thing." I have hoped to write a book that would help all of us—in our own loneliness, or in our desire to reach out to those who are lonely.

This is not a book by a professional Lonelinessist or Lonely-ist (can't figure out how to spell it). I guess there really isn't such a profession, but I just want to make sure you don't choose this book because you think it will give you, finally, the answers to exactly what causes loneliness and exactly what cures it. It just is *not* a "scientific" book.

It *is* a book that will offer lots of suggestions and lots of hope. Loneliness is a terrible, painful thing, but it's not terminal.

It can be lessened. This book holds some thoughts I hope may be helpful to any who struggle with feelings of loneliness, and any who wish to help.

One of the things I struggled with most may have been coming up with the title. *Buck Up, Little Buckaroo!* started out as a title I was only going to use until I could think of something better. I wasn't sure I liked that title because it felt like it made light of something that is very real and very painful (loneliness can certainly be both). One strong impression I had was that to discount loneliness is to become unable to help or understand. But in the end I decided that the cheerful hope in the title made it all right. After all, one of the things I hope people will take away from this book is that, as hard as it is, loneliness doesn't need to rule our lives. There is so much happiness available to us, not just in eternity but right here and right now!

I have felt all along that I've been writing the book for YOU. I don't know who you are, but you've been on my mind, in my heart, and in my prayers as I've worked hard to write something that will be meaningful to you—not just comforting, although I hope it will be, but helpful in some specific ways.

I tried to make it so there wasn't anything in here that would encourage anyone to hang on to loneliness. I hope we can learn to let others know when we're feeling alone and lonely. Isn't it sad that we often shut others out and thus add to our loneliness?

There's one chapter that's pure nonsense. I couldn't help

myself. There's nothing funny about loneliness, but I needed a place for my imagination to go wild. If you're not in a silly mood, you may want to skip that chapter. You'll know which chapter it is when you get there.

When I thought of sharing some of my own experiences as I began writing, it made me uncomfortable. I thought, "Well, I've not really suffered anything worth mentioning." I've not had many of the same experiences *you've* had. But there *are* some things that have been difficult for me, and that I might remember as involving some degree of loneliness. I wanted to share enough so that you could be with me, feel with me, and understand. I hope my experiences have helped me to feel empathy and compassion for those who struggle so much with feeling alone and lonely. I think those who know me and read this will realize that I've managed to keep pretty optimistic and happy through all my years.

I'm so thankful for all those in my life who help me to be less lonely, and that includes all who have helped with this book—those who have listened to my ideas, responded to my questions, shared their hearts, and given me encouragement. I'm sending a special "shout out" to Leanne and her family, with extra thanks to Jon and all the children and grandchildren for being so generous in letting Leanne help me so significantly with this book and other projects, and for cheering on our amazing friendship. Thank you!

I'm exceedingly grateful for the wonderful team at Deseret Book who asked if I would give this a try and have spiffed up the rough draft I gave them to make it so much better than it was. Thanks to Jana, Emily, and all others who know how to do things that I'm not even aware of to make a rough draft into a book.

Some of the royalties from this book will go toward defeating breast cancer. I have friends who have been taken away, and I have friends who have "beat it." I want to help increase this second group. The fight against cancer can be a lonely journey. Thanks for contributing through your purchase!

Chapter 1

What is Loneliness?

Blessed are ye that hunger now: for ye shall be filled.
Blessed are ye that weep now: for ye shall laugh.

Luke 6:21

One of my first experiences with loneliness that lingered was when I was seventeen years old and our family moved away from Cedar City, Utah. I'll remember forever driving away from our home, our friends, our neighborhood, our wonderful community. I felt like life was over. I remember thinking I would never be happy again.

Whenever I read my diary from this part of my life, I feel so bad for my younger self. I really poured out my feelings. Everything was strange and unfamiliar. I felt so very lonely.

But this move from my hometown would eventually seem relatively trouble-free. I'm not discounting my previous experiences and feelings, but they were trumped by what happened to me when I was twenty-two years old and was called on a mission.

I can illustrate how much of a homebody I was by telling you that when I received this first mission call in 1962 to the "Southern Far East," for a moment I thought I was going to Florida! It makes me smile to know that I wasn't the only one in our family to have such an experience. When one of my younger sisters, Susan, received her mission call several years later, she saw "Central America" and asked, "Oh! Which states are those?"

Suffice it to say that I grew up in a very small world. I hadn't been far from home and family on very many occasions for any length of time.

And then it happened. "Southern Far East" turned out to be Asia! The mission president was located in Hong Kong, and that was where I headed. I traveled as far as I could go without starting home again—halfway around the globe.

And OH! I was so LONELY! So much that was new and different hit me all at once. So THIS was culture shock: the unknown!

I stepped off the plane and felt like I'd stepped directly into a sauna. Wasn't I supposed to be able to breathe?

I heard all these noises and realized that people were using them to communicate. Even little children! The tones of their Cantonese made it sound like some kind of a song or chant. This was a language?

People drove on the other side of the road, so steering wheels were on the other side of all the vehicles. Can you imagine the adjustment after a lifetime of looking a certain way to see if there were cars coming? More than once or twice I was scared half to death by one of the double-decker busses being in the wrong place.

The buildings were so tall, filling every little inch of space. There were very few yards that I could see. And the people . . . there were SO MANY PEOPLE! I had never in all my born days seen that many people all at once. It was so crowded! No "personal space" at all.

I remember thinking that I couldn't have felt more alone or any more separated from my family and everything familiar if I had landed on the moon or Mars!

How did I overcome that terrible loneliness? With time. With learning slowly but surely how to communicate. With a wonderful companion named Jan Bair. With a blessing from my mission president. With the friendship of many kind people in the city of Tainan in Taiwan, where I was first assigned. And mostly with the kindness of a loving Heavenly Father.

I do have to add that when I got sick and had to be transferred to Hong Kong right after Christmas, I felt lonely for Taiwan! And after five fascinating, adventurous months in Hong Kong, I was transferred to the Philippines, and I missed Hong Kong AND Taiwan. And when it was time for me to leave the Philippines and return home, I was positive I would die. As lonely as I had been in each of those places for a time, the priceless experiences I had there soon outweighed those lonely feelings.

What *is* loneliness? How does it feel, and how do we describe those feelings?

Simply put, loneliness means being alone—or *feeling* alone—when you don't want to be. It's unwanted solitude. It can start small and build, or it can happen suddenly, unexpectedly, for no apparent reason. It can be very real and very painful. Even the word *loneliness* sounds . . . well . . . alone.

I mention both being alone and feeling alone because you don't have to be alone to be lonely. If you've ever felt lonely in a crowd, you know what I mean. One person I talked to said she feels especially lonely at family reunions. Some said they feel lonely at Christmastime or on other holidays, or on their birthdays. Some feel lonely at church meetings or activities or on a plane or train or bus, at a ball game or rodeo, at the beach or a parade or a play or a concert.

I've asked many people what loneliness feels like to them, how they would describe it. The words and phrases they use are varied. One of the most common words was "painful." Other expressions included "feeling lost," "like a light's gone out," "a constant empty place inside," "exclusion," "having no sense of time," "a feeling of nothingness," "friendless," "not belonging," "having no control," "futility," "rejection," "an inescapable reality," "feeling abandoned."

Wow. When I read through that list, I can hardly stand to think that some people feel lonely almost all the time!

I don't think I've talked to anyone (and I've talked to a lot of people) who has not had times of loneliness in his or her life.

Please realize that almost everyone gets lonely, even if some don't recognize that's what they're feeling. It doesn't mean there is anything wrong with them. Being lonely at times seems to be part of life, and even the friendliest and most outgoing of people experience those feelings.

Being lonely isn't necessarily bad for you, but *staying* lonely is. It's a dangerous illness. It is a disease in the fullest sense of the word. Loneliness has been linked to heart disease and premature aging as well as emotional problems such as anxiety and depression. Loneliness can interfere with learning and memory skills. People who are extremely lonely may be unable to perform even the simplest acts of daily living. Anyone who is experiencing unmanageable loneliness needs to get some help as quickly as possible.

Some say that loneliness is more than just the feeling of wanting to feel needed, wanting company, or wanting to do something with another person. It's a desire—a need—to feel connected, to feel that you matter to someone, that someone loves you and cares about you.

One man said that when his wife died, he was absolutely devastated. He felt like he would never again come "first" with anyone. He could hardly stand the loneliness. Some of his friends expected him to get over his loss pretty quickly, but his feeling was, "How can I respond the way they want me to when I still listen for her footsteps in the house . . . when I'm waiting to hear her voice, or her breathing coming from her chair?"

It's as if it hurts to feel lonely in the first place, and then it hurts even more because there's no one to share it with.

Some say they have such mixed emotions when they're feeling desperately alone and lonely. They say they feel like they've shut their door, locked it, bolted it, and put out the "Do Not Disturb" sign. And yet inside they are crying out for someone, anyone, to come ANYWAY!

Maybe loneliness is different for you from how it is for someone close to you. Please let's not turn this into a comparison, as we tend to do with so many things. "Well, if you think YOU'RE lonely, you ought to feel how I feel! I'll bet MY loneliness is ten times worse than yours! I'll bet I've cried a million more tears than you have! I'm positive you don't hurt as bad as I do. You can't even begin to know how much I loved Billy Bob!"

Okay, I've exaggerated . . . but sometimes we may accidentally or intentionally try to discount others' loneliness. We feel certain that our feelings are the most painful.

I'm wondering if YOU have ever felt lonely. Maybe not. What a nice blessing if you never have. But I actually feel it is unrealistic for us to expect to escape all feelings of loneliness, whether we are alone or with other people.

If you're not sure whether you've ever felt lonely, maybe you could ask yourself some questions:

- Do you remember the first time you were away from home, or the first time you ran away from home?
- Did you ever have a best friend move away?

What Is Loneliness?

- Do you ever feel sad and like you don't have anyone you can talk to—no one you can pour out your heart to who will really listen and try to understand?

- Were you ever a freshman at college with new room-mates and a lot to adjust to?

- Have you ever been through a divorce?

- Can you think of any kind of transition you've made where you've needed to look for people who shared your interests and thoughts?

- Did you have a new baby and there was no one around to help you, to teach and show you what to do?

- Have there ever been times when you could hardly stand being alone or doing things alone (going to a movie, a party, a meeting, a parade, to church, or to some other function)?

- Have you had or are you now having the experience of being a single parent?

- Are there days when you wish someone would call or send an e-mail or a text or a smoke signal or SOMETHING?

- Has there ever been a time when it's been hard for you to reach out to others, even those closest to you?

- Is it ever hard for you to make friends?

- Have you served in the military, or are you in that circumstance now?

- Have there been times when you've pulled away from

the Church, from the gospel, and maybe even from your Heavenly Father, and you've felt a deep sense of loneliness?

- Have you lost a parent? A child? Some other dear one?

- Have you been on a mission and experienced homesickness?

- Is there anything you're having trouble dealing with?

- Have you ever felt alone even when you were "surrounded"—at a store, an airport, a state fair, any kind of activity or celebration?

- Have you ever felt excluded from a group you wanted to be part of?

- Have you ever picked up the phone to call someone who wasn't there anymore? Many of us do that after our parents have gone Home.

- Have you ever wondered, "Is anybody there for me?"

Loneliness is sometimes almost forced upon us. We may find ourselves in a situation where it's almost impossible NOT to feel lonely. There are so many things that can cause loneliness. There are probably as many causes as there are people.

I've done a lot of thinking about what causes loneliness. Though it's not a topic anyone would want to dwell on for too long, sometimes just recognizing what things might be contributing to our loneliness can be a catalyst to help us make some changes.

I think being separated from those you love dearly, for

whatever reason, is one of the major causes. Friends and neighbors I've talked to through the years who have lost a spouse or other loved one, for example, describe such longing, such a sense of loss, such loneliness.

One thing that causes me to experience occasional feelings of loneliness is not having someone to talk to much of the time. It would be so nice to come home and have someone waiting to hear all about my day, my trip, my adventure, my "boring stuff." I try to write some of it down, but that's not the same as having someone listening—seeing their face, hearing them laugh, feeling their response to what I share, and hearing their questions and comments. I like to come home after I've been gone for a while and call out things like, "Why doesn't anybody *do* anything around here while I'm gone?"

What about you—can you think of some possible causes for the loneliness you may feel or have felt? Maybe you've experienced some of the following things, any of which could make you feel lonely:

Having the burden of a confidence that you can't share with anyone. Grief. Being a leader. Having trouble adequately expressing your feelings, ideas, experiences, concerns. Chronic illness. Feeling shy and unable to reach out to other people (shyness and loneliness seem pretty closely associated). Changes in life patterns. Being the only single person among friends or family. Not feeling important. Sitting in a meeting where it's once again more about families than about the Savior. Having a husband (or a wife) whose Church calling keeps them away a lot. Traveling a lot and being away from family and other loved ones. Anger. The perception but not the reality of belonging to a group—you are invited to be in a book club or attend an activity, but you don't really feel part of the group. The loss of a significant person in your life.

Loneliness is not caused by being alone so much as by being without something that you desperately need, especially meaningful relationships.

I know mothers of young children who would love to spend more time communicating with those who are able to talk in sentences, and some who almost wish they had raised children before seat belts and car seats were invented (it used to be so easy to just "toss the kids in" and take off in the car). And I know parents of teenagers who think it must have been so much easier to be a parent before texting, Facebook, the Internet, solo bedrooms, video games, and so on. "I never see my son! I never really have a chance to talk to him! Even when I think I'm talking to him, he's texting his friends under the table!"

There are times when people are put in a position of having to make major decisions, and that can be a lonely situation. President Ezra Taft Benson quoted a friend, Clarence Randall, as saying, "Decision making is a lonely business, and the greater the degree of responsibility, the more intense the loneliness" (God, Family, Country: Our Three Great Loyalties, 150–51).

Sin can create loneliness, and it can also bring fear. If there are things in our lives which we haven't resolved, or we're living and behaving contrary to our deepest beliefs, we can feel separated from God and also from others.

Loneliness can come when we are released from a calling, or when we retire from our profession, our job. When I was released in 1997 from the general board of the Relief Society after eleven years, I missed the regular association with great, wonderful women who had become dear friends. And when I retired from the Missionary Training Center in 1995 after close to twenty years, I thought I would be back often to see everyone, to keep closely in touch. I wasn't prepared for the awful feeling of going there and not belonging anymore! For several years I still went on Sundays to teach the sister missionaries, but very seldom were there any of the friends, the colleagues, with whom I'd worked so closely for so many years. It was an "ouch" I hadn't anticipated.

Health challenges can certainly contribute to loneliness. I'm certain that you could add some important examples from your own life as well as the lives of those you love.

One type of such health-related loneliness began annoying me around the turn of the century. (It feels quite exotic to say that—to have experienced it.) I noticed that my hearing wasn't as great as it had been for all the years up to that point.

It's so frustrating and discouraging not to be able to hear well. I sit in meetings, particularly when people in the group are sharing ideas and experiences, and I feel so distanced from everything and everyone. I get tired of saying "Excuse me?" "Pardon me?" "Once more, please." Things like that. "EH???"

Yes, I have hearing aids, and I have no "fashion problem" in wearing them. It's just that for the most part they magnify all noises. It can rattle my brain to have someone shut a door, close a book, sneeze, cough, or have a baby squeal or cry.

It's frustrating that although noises are made louder, there is not the distinguishing what is being said which came with my ears in my birth-day package so many years ago. I have learned more about the miracle of ears since losing much of my ability to hear and understand.

In recent years I entered a season of life where I have limited energy due to COPD (chronic obstructive pulmonary disease). Too many years in hot, humid climates (think Taiwan, Hong Kong, Philippines, Indonesia, and Africa).

I remember asking my doctor, "Will I be this way until Jesus comes?" He said yes. So I asked, "Well, when's He coming?" My doctor didn't know (or I'd have told all of you).

This is a major change for me, and a difficult adjustment. Whoever would have believed this former world-class athlete (okay, that's a huge exaggeration, but I really WAS very active and healthy most of my life) would have a handicapped parking thingie? Not MEE!

So far I don't have to use it very often, but when I do, I'm so thankful to have it. I still find it awkward. Maybe people looking at me are thinking, "She's old, but she looks like she's moving pretty well." I want to shout, "LUNGS, not LEGS!" Snort.

It's a "given," I think, that there will be an increase in

loneliness as our population grows older—people are living longer and are spending long periods of time alone (like in widowhood). And old people will not go away! I'M certainly not going away!

I think the unknown can be a cause of fear and loneliness. Sometimes we "fill in the blank" of that which is unknown in our lives. I call this "coming up with the what-ifs." This may happen especially for those who have a vivid imagination. I've been blessed with one of those. My mind can have you dead and gone if you're even a few minutes late.

Do you know what I mean? Has there ever been a time when you didn't know where a loved one was? Maybe he or she was in a place where there had been a fire or a flood, an earthquake or a typhoon, a snowstorm or a car accident, and you couldn't get in touch with someone very dear to you. Do you remember how that felt?

On Tuesday, September 25, 1984, and into the next morning, I had such an experience, and it was one of the longest and loneliest nights of my life.

I was in Nigeria, West Africa. My companion, Ann, and I had just arrived a few weeks earlier to begin a health project for children.

Rob from our headquarters office in Salt Lake City had come with us, and it was time for him to return home. I was too sick to go along to the airport, so Ann left with one of our wonderful missionary couple neighbors to make the journey from our home in the village of Eket to the airport in Calabar.

They would be back in the afternoon—we had a rule in the mission that we wouldn't be out after dark. When there's no electricity, dark is REALLY dark. I was staying with another missionary couple to wait for Ann's return. They had some work to do outside of the home, and so I was alone. I had a lot of time to think as I waited.

As it got darker, I began to feel some concern. I sat near a window so I could see Ann and our neighbors arrive. I kept watching. Waiting. Time passed. It was dark and quiet and I really started to worry. I knew there had been plenty of time—a whole day—for them to get to Calabar and back. I tried to keep calm, but it wasn't working.

The couple I was staying with finally got home. We were all concerned, and yet we realized it would be unwise to try to find the others in the dark with no idea of which roads they may have taken.

I felt so helpless! I wanted to do something—to search for them, to make sure they were all right! The only option I had was to continue praying earnestly, and to wait.

We prepared our simple dinner, and I set a place for Ann. I tried to eat slowly, thinking I could have a little bit left to eat when Ann got back so she wouldn't have to eat alone.

But eventually we finished and cleared the table. Except that I couldn't clear Ann's place. I couldn't explain it, but I had to leave her place there. It was as if by doing so I was saying, "She'll be home any minute; let's save her a place and something to eat. She'll be hungry."

After a while they cleared her place.

I helped wash the dishes, but other than that I just sat by the window watching for the lights of the car. Each time some lights would approach, I would plead with them to be the lights I was looking for. *Please turn into our compound. Please come over here. Please be Ann and our neighbors. Please don't pass by.* But they did. They all passed by.

It's hard to describe adequately how I felt—helpless, frightened, frustrated, and so terribly lonely. Why didn't we have a telephone so we could call around and ask the couples in Calabar if they'd seen our friends? I've never called 911 in my life, but this was a time when I desperately wanted to do just that. Oh, how I was wishing we had telephones in our village! Telephones that worked!

It got completely dark, and I decided I'd better try to get some sleep, especially since I was so sick. But I was torn—I didn't want to "abandon" Ann. Part of me felt like it was important to keep watching and waiting.

My imagination went wild. Sometimes I would imagine that maybe Ann was hurt—that there'd been a terrible accident or something, and she was calling to me, needing my help, and I wasn't there. The "not knowing" was the hardest thing.

I've never spent a night quite like that in my whole life. It was awful—one of the most awful experiences I have ever endured. I kept realizing that the only thing I could do (beyond letting my imagination run away too far to call it back) was to pray—to plead with Heavenly Father to watch over my friends and to somehow bring some peace to my heart and help me to get the sleep and rest I so much needed.

My communication with Heavenly Father was so *real* all during that time. There were no trite phrases or unplanned ramblings. And there was no thought of a brief prayer that would end after a few minutes. I needed Him *all night,* and I knew it. There was no one else to talk to. He was watching over all of us—me in my dark little room and them wherever they were, even if they were with Him at that moment. I worked hard at pouring out what I was *really* feeling, including my awareness of His help and kindness through the whole process of getting ready to come to Africa, arriving, and starting our work. *Please,* I asked, *please just let them come back safely and let us continue with what we've begun.*

The next morning I was so exhausted, both physically and emotionally, that I could hardly get up and going. I wasn't in the mood to do much.

I went next door to the home Ann and I were supposed to be moving into soon. I wanted to be alone with my helplessness and my constant prayers. I was sick inside and out. I had decided that the best thing I could do would be to get to work—to be so busy that I'd calm down my imagination somewhat.

Then I heard the car drive in. I was afraid to look out to make sure that was who it was. I kept holding my breath and walking around, wringing my hands together and pleading aloud, "Let it be them. Let it be Ann. Let them be safe. Please let them be home finally." On and on. And then there she was, whole and well and tired and real and alive. I hugged her and cried and cried. I couldn't even begin to ask any questions or share my feelings. I was more grateful than I could or can put into words.

We were eventually able to tell each other about our "longest night," when we had both been thinking of each other. She said it was so hard for her, knowing that I'd be terribly worried but not having any way in the world of communicating with me.

She reported that they got to Calabar, got Rob to the airport, ran some errands, and then headed back. The car had been heating up and stopping, and eventually it just stopped and wouldn't start again.

Some people came to help. One man seemed to know something about cars, so Ann asked, "Are you a mechanic?" and he responded "yes" with a tone like, "Well, of course I am—God is watching out for you, isn't He?"

This kind man worked all afternoon—from about three o'clock until around nine in the evening. The family insisted that Ann and our neighbors stay the night with them, that it was too dangerous to be out on the roads. They pushed the car over beside their little home to keep it safe. And they all slept on the floor in their clothes.

And so the long, long night that seemed like it would *never* end finally did, and we were back together, more conscious than ever of our isolation and lack of ability to communicate in an earthly way, but so thankful for the blessing of protection and safety.

I share that experience because I think it teaches several important lessons about loneliness. It shows how connected loneliness and fear can be, especially fear of the unknown. Most important, though, it shows how reliant we can and must be on our Heavenly Father to see us through our times of loneliness.

Is loneliness a bad thing? If we're not able to handle it, it certainly can be. But maybe in some sense it could be a good thing—maybe we have more love when there is loneliness to inspire it.

President Spencer W. Kimball taught: "Being human, we would expel from our lives physical pain and mental anguish and assure ourselves of continual ease and comfort, but if we were to close the doors upon sorrow and distress, we might be excluding our greatest friends and benefactors. Suffering can make saints of people as they learn patience, long-suffering, and self-mastery" (*Faith Precedes the Miracle*, 98).

There are times when I probably would do just that—get rid of the things in my life that have taught me the greatest blessings and left the deepest and sweetest impressions of God's mercy and tenderness on and in my soul.

I'm aware of feelings I have sometimes of wanting "quick cures," and wanting to get rid of all the trials and tribulations that surround me and everyone. I've thought at times that if I were in charge, there may not be any hospitals or funerals.

President John Taylor, who experienced a great deal of

suffering, said: "I used to think, if I were the Lord, I would not suffer people to be tried as they are; but I have changed my mind on that subject. Now I think I would, if I were the Lord, because it purges out the meanness and corruption that stick around the Saints, like flies around molasses" (*Journal of Discourses,* 5:115).

We probably will not escape feeling lonely at some time in our lives. That seems to be part of the mortal experience, maybe even part of our refining process. We are social animals, and we need each other. We have a basic need to connect with others, to feel that we belong, to feel that others care about where we are and how we are, and that we are cherished and understood. We have need for support, for love. Our bodies get hungry, and our souls do too. And it is often our loneliness that creates our soul hunger.

Maybe we NEED this hunger in our souls. It may be what pushes us toward heaven and toward our Heavenly Father, who is always there. He and the Savior will not leave us comfortless. They will never leave us absolutely alone. Remembering that single truth may be what gets us through those times of loneliness that will likely come our way.

~ Chapter 2 ~

Strategies for Dealing with Loneliness

Loud may the sound
Of hope ring till all doubt departs,
And we are bound
To him by loving ties.
"Our Savior's Love," *Hymns,* no. 113

H ow do we cope with our loneliness? How have others done it—not just surviving but actually overcoming some of their deepest loneliness?

Although there are no easy answers regarding what to do about loneliness, making a determined effort to help yourself is the place to start. What is it YOU do to assuage some of your feelings of loneliness? How and where do you find a drink of cool water in a hot desert time of your life? What are some strategies that may help lessen the length, breadth, height, and depth of loneliness?

I've presented a list of ideas below that I hope you will find helpful. Consider them and see if there are any that would be possible and meaningful for you in your present circumstances. Remember, not every suggestion works for all of the forty-two people who will read this book. Try one or two strategies and see what works for you. Something that is effective this time may not work in the future, so keep the list handy.

Creating a list like this is a challenge, because we're lonely for different reasons. Some people are lonely because they are single; others feel isolated in their roles as mothers with small children. I've thought of those who have lost spouses and are now living alone. I've thought of men who've been widowed who don't know how to cook any better than I do. (Yikes!) I've thought of single parents. I've thought of new missionaries, students away from home at school, men and women in the military, far from home . . .

And depending on who's on my mind, I've thought, "I can't put this idea in here—it would be discouraging and frustrating for them even to read it, let alone try to do it."

So keep that in mind. There will be things that just do NOT relate to you in your current season. Just skip things that you are pretty sure won't be possible or helpful for you right now. Maybe in a few years? (Or maybe never.)

Here, then, are some ideas, and I hope you can find at least one or two things to which you can say, "I think that would help me!" They are not in alphabetical order, nor are they in order of importance.

As You Can, Cut Down on Things That Make You Feel Anxious and Lonely

I put "as you can," because maybe someone would like to cut out all laundry or housekeeping or diaper changing or meal fixing or commuting or something like that. With some things it's hard even to cut down, let alone cut out! And there are probably times when you feel powerless to do anything to change your situation. So: "As you can."

Lonely is as lonely does. Sometimes we're our own worst enemy . . . our own loneliness-causer.

Be conscious of times when you're trapped in negative thinking, and challenge those thoughts. Ask yourself questions that will bring forth your common sense. Remind yourself that although it isn't fun being alone, there could be worse things. What if you were living with someone you couldn't stand?

Consider a few things (and then add to your own list): Would it help to cut down on watching or reading depressing things? Maybe like the news?

See if you can tell that watching certain programs or reading certain articles in magazines or the newspaper or online makes you feel helpless, angry, frustrated, or sad. Can you cut down on the "dose"? Can you find some balance? Can you find a source for good news, for positive outcomes, for "happy endings"?

Recognize That Ultimately You Are the Source of Your Happiness or Unhappiness

I saw a "Peanuts" cartoon once where Lucy is wearing her frowny face, and she says something like, "Whoever is in charge of my happiness isn't doing a good job!" Hopefully someone, maybe Snoopy, let her know that SHE was the one in charge of her own happiness.

We never need to be ashamed or feel guilty about feelings of loneliness—but we do have to fight them. President David O. McKay and others have taught that some of our greatest battles are fought within our own hearts and souls. The battle to conquer feelings of loneliness isn't easy, and there may be relapses. At times it can feel like loneliness is more powerful than we are. But we can succeed if we try hard to participate in meaningful activities and to avoid anger, self-pity, and criticism.

We can't wait for happiness until someone comes along who we believe can make us happy. Choose happiness. Make a conscious choice to be happy. Work at it. Nurture it. Associate with people who happify you, and see if you can become a happifier.

We can each become our own best friend by doing things that we enjoy and treating ourselves well. We can treat ourselves now as we would like others to treat us.

Being alone doesn't have to mean that we are unhappy, though we can certainly make it that way if we're not careful. Take it one day at a time and stay committed in trying to solve your problems and find happiness. Consciously decide to work at making yourself a better, happier person.

Record Your Thoughts

I find this pretty therapeutic. I don't know that it snaps me out of my loneliness, but for some reason it helps—writing down how I feel, exploring the why, and describing what's going on in my life. Just by doing that I sometimes find a possible solution, a key to getting out of my "funk," a reason for my loneliness that I can do something about. And even when that doesn't happen—times when I can't really find a "cure"—I almost always feel better anyway, just having told the computer or the paper how I'm feeling. Just writing about your loneliness may turn out to be very helpful to you and to others.

Write Letters and Notes

Sometimes it has helped me in significant ways to write letters and notes to people. I use e-mail a lot, especially early in the morning when a phone call would be irritating to the person I've chosen to call.

Write to a missionary or someone else who is far from home and might be lonely. Tell them of some of your funny and/or interesting experiences.

Sometimes I write letters that I don't send—have you ever tried that? There's such freedom in being absolutely honest without worrying how someone is going to react or respond . . . because you may never give them the letter.

24

Go for a Walk

Do you live in an area where you can safely go for a walk? I'm glad I'm able to walk in the great out-of-doors (most of the time), hearing birds and seeing the beauty in nature. Some people walk in a mall or at a local health club or fitness center. When I walk, I think and ponder. I pray. I sort out things. Many people walk with others—a spouse, a neighbor, a friend. Whatever works!

Look at Loneliness as a Positive Signal

There are times when loneliness can be a positive thing. It can let us know when it is time to reach outside ourselves for new friends and opportunities or to strengthen our existing relationships. A deep, lasting relationship can make such a difference in life.

Have Your Home Dedicated

One thing that has helped me immeasurably has been the blessing of having my home dedicated. (The mortgage does not need to be paid off completely in order for this to happen, according to the Church's Handbook, available on lds.org.) In Mapleton it was my Dad who did that, and in American Fork it was my youngest brother, Richard. If you haven't yet done this, I highly recommend it as a source of an increased sense of peace, safety, and comfort—even for those of you who don't live alone.

Find a Hobby or Make One Up

Is there something you enjoy collecting? Stamps? Coins? Rubber bands? Christmas ornaments? Fabric? Memories? Is there something you enjoy doing? Making dresses for dolls or arranging flowers? Playing golf or Ping-Pong? Riding your bike or your motorcycle? Or your scooter? Puttering in your garden or your basement? Having a hobby can make time pass instead of drag, and that can lift your spirits.

Adopt or Borrow a Pet

If this is something you'd enjoy, and you're not allergic to dogs, cats, guinea pigs, exotic birds, goldfish, little dragons, or anything else you might choose, this could make a big difference for you. Animals can make marvelous companions; they give unconditional love and can offer you loyal company.

Animals have been used in what is called "pet therapy." I remember the excitement when my mother took two of her St. Bernards (she raised Bernards for several years) to a care center—I think the owners and staff were pretty excited about that! (She hadn't asked for permission.) Our "Aunt Florence" loved the change in routine!

Walking a dog (or bunny rabbit, wombat, or dinosaur) can also be a great way of meeting other people! Maybe you could just volunteer to take a neighbor's dog or raccoon for a walk— that way you're not responsible for feeding, cleaning, vet visits, and so forth. Up to you.

Work on Puzzles or Games

As a break and a way of exercising your mind (in addition to chasing away some of your loneliness), try working on puzzles or playing some games. Invite someone to come and play Parcheesi, marbles, Old Maid, or hopscotch. This may lead to a strengthened friendship and a lessening of loneliness. Engage yourself in some activity that keeps your mind occupied.

Count Your Many Blessings

And yes, name them one by one. Not only will it surprise you what the Lord has done, but it will help you to feel loved by your Heavenly Father. Focusing on what we DO have—how blessed we are—can remind us of how much we're noticed and cherished.

Think of Strategies Ahead of Time

Make yourself a list. Write down things that help you feel better. If you feel yourself sinking, look at your list and see if you can find something that has worked in the past and may work again. "Walk around the block." "Find the cartoon collection." "Play the harmonica." "Call Elise." "Dance in the hall." "Make a smoothie." "Send a funny card to Anna." "Clean a drawer." "Reread the note from Wendy." "Put fresh batteries in the smoke alarm."

Add to your list as you find new, increasingly effective strategies.

Have Things to Look Forward To

This is one of my favorites. When I'm anticipating something I'm going to enjoy, I can say to myself, "Just make it through this hour (or this day, or this experience), and then POW! You can do this!"

And I don't think you have to have huge things to look forward to, like a trip to the Grand Canyon or a ride on a space shuttle. They can be small things, just as long as you really do look forward to them.

These can overlap with your list of strategies. But the strategies are mostly about breaking the cycle of loneliness, about doing something different. Having things to look forward to means you don't do them right now. You anticipate them, you make some plans—like going to a movie or a play, or driving up the canyon next Thursday, or going to visit someone on their birthday.

Go to Sleep

One of the times when I feel lonely is in the late afternoon. I seem to sink with the sun. The way I deal with that is to go to bed. As you might guess, in the wintertime that tends to be very early. VERY early. And if I'm being honest, I really don't make huge changes when summer comes.

Somehow my brain knows that in the evening it's going to get darker, but when I get up in the morning (also VERY early), even though it's pitch dark, my brain knows it's going to gradually get lighter. It always does.

Many people use sleep to try to escape their loneliness. I realize that can get to be too much—if we're not careful, we could be sleeping our lives away. I guess we just hope that when we wake up, things will be better; and often they are.

Have Interesting Things to Study

Another thing I do that is helpful when I can feel a wave of loneliness headed my direction is to have something to study. I keep a list of things I want to learn more about. I have a curious mind, and I really enjoy learning. This may not be your "cup of herbal tea," but try it if you think it would help.

Some of the things on my to-study list are: spiritual self-reliance, Challenger Deep in the Pacific Ocean, Apophis, how pearls are made, George Q. Cannon, multiverse (kind of sounds like poetry, doesn't it, but it's astrophysics), Perpetuum Jazzile, Jose Rizal, galaxies . . . I think you can tell that I have a VERY long list.

I just have to say that I am so grateful for Google!

Avoid False Cures

Oh, friends . . . sometimes when we're feeling lonely, un-loved, and even unlovable, we may turn to things that aren't good for us. Loneliness is such a painful, frightening experience that most people will do practically anything to avoid it. We may turn to behaviors that actually increase our loneliness in-stead of relieving it.

We may try to cover up our loneliness by overeating,

sleeping more than is needful, taking tranquilizers, filling our minds with things that don't nourish our souls by spending inordinate amounts of time watching "nothing" on TV or "surfing the net" without any particular meaningful goal in mind. Some may go shopping and spend a lot of money (that alone drops this idea from my list of possibilities).

Be careful. Don't get to a point where you indulge in drugs, alcohol, or any other substance or activity that could become a very unhealthy addiction. There are things worse than feeling lonely.

Get to Know Your Neighbors

Even if you don't become best friends, it can be so helpful and comforting to know that someone close to you is aware of you and that there is mutual concern. Lend a hand to each other. Put their newspaper up on the porch. Let them know of a rogue sprinkler head. Forge some ties. If you live in an apartment building or an assisted-care center, leave a surprise at someone's door. Look for others who share your interests.

Smile and Say Hello

Say hello to a neighbor or shopkeeper you see frequently. Develop a community of friends—one friend at a time.

Since I've moved from a place where I knew and was known by practically everyone, I've made it a point to talk to people in the places where I go most frequently. Gaye at the bank. Dale at the place where I get my car serviced. And I like the anticipation of knowing Gary at Costco will laugh when he sees me coming, and will say things like, "How'd YOU get in? Our security sure isn't working!" Or of having Raymond at the grocery store ask, "Are you still happy?" It's nice to feel like someone in the places where we go recognizes us and may even know our name.

Have a Good Cry

Sometimes, but hopefully not all the time, it helps to have a good cry. Sooner or later, for most of us, the pain of loneliness is accompanied by tears.

Several months after my mother died, I was praying before going to bed, and I'd been feeling unusually lonely. I told Heavenly Father about that, and then added that I really, really missed my mother. It was as if I'd taken my finger out of the dike. I cried so hard! It was as if I'd saved it all up for this moment, and out it came. I felt better afterwards, as though I had needed to cry.

Appreciate Your Friends

Some individuals refuse to use their friends for comfort or solace when they are blue. They search futilely for someone new to take their lonely feelings away. Usually, however, when people are feeling down, their capacity to form new relationships is low, and this leads to more desperate feelings of loneliness and frustration. Strive to cultivate and appreciate the friends you already have. It is such a great blessing to have someone who can give us a sense of safety and security, who can tell us that everything is going to be all right.

Be Realistic

No one will totally escape experiencing feelings of loneliness from time to time. Let us learn to accept them as natural and sometimes helpful signals about where we are in life.

Loneliness need not be overwhelming if we keep a realistic perspective about feeling lonely, cultivate the skill of enjoying time alone, and build relationships that can offer comfort and support.

Listen More Than Talk

Listening and drawing people out will deepen your contacts more than just talking endlessly about yourself.

Read a Good Book

In addition to the scriptures, find something you'd enjoy reading.

Say No When You Need To

I guess I should also add that we ought to say yes when we need to. I was thinking of no because it occurred to me that sometimes others will ask you to do things with them, meaning to be kind and helpful, and they are things you just can't do or don't wish to do.

For example, let's say you're newly widowed, and

well-meaning friends invite you to spend Christmas with them—but it's too soon, and you need more time. Don't be afraid to say no sometimes.

Get the Rest You Need

Do what you can to accomplish this, including a nap or two during the day if you need that and if it's possible. I can think of people I know who would say to me, "I'd LOVE to take a nap! I'd LOVE to sleep longer at night! I'd LOVE to get to bed earlier and get up later than I have to!"

I wish I could wrap up an hour or two and send them to you. I really mean that. Except I'd really miss them.

But I still say do what you can to get the sleep and rest you need. Fatigue adds to loneliness (and to frustration, short tempers, and lots of other "maladies").

Let Others Know You're Lonely

Inform family and friends that you're lonely. We often assume that they know and don't care. In reality, they may be surprised to learn what we're feeling. Don't languish in loneliness. Let someone know. Too often we try to hide it (by hiding ourselves and getting lonelier).

Speak up if you can. Sharing your distress with another person could ease it. It's helpful to talk to others about your loneliness, not to complain or wallow, but to search for solutions.

Let Others Help You

Accept the kindness of others. Sometimes it's easy not to accept an invitation because you think the person is offering "just to be nice." If the person is thoughtful enough to offer, accept and be grateful.

Maybe it doesn't seem helpful when someone says to you, "Let me know if I can do anything to help you." But when someone says that to you, write down his or her name and telephone number, and as you think of something that really *would* help, call and ask. Let the person help you. I know this is NOT EASY for most of us. It may not even be pleasant. But it could be that these experiences will produce some miracles, maybe including a new friendship or a stronger relationship with someone who is already your friend. If you're not sure how a person can help you, just call and say, "I need you," and then maybe you can list 17 or 23 things on your list of things that needed to be done last month and see if there's anything he or she can do.

Include Your Children in Planning

If you still have children at home, even if they're small, let them help make some decisions that will lighten your burdens and lessen your feelings of loneliness. One underused avenue I'm thinking of is family councils.

Are any of your children old enough to recognize what it means to be lonely? Can you explain to them that sometimes you feel that way? I have a feeling that your honesty and openness could make a difference. Let them know it's not their fault.

Even if part of your loneliness is because you have heavy burdens with all that is on your shoulders, I doubt children set out to make their parents feel lonely. Maybe frustrated and screaming, but not lonely.

Find Someone Lonelier Than You Are

I'm not saying this will be easy, but I'm pretty sure it will be possible. This is not one where you can look in the Yellow Pages. You have to look into hearts—yours and others. Do your best to turn outward, not inward.

Remember that reaching out to someone else lonelier than you could give you more happiness than you could imagine.

Reaching out to a lonely person is one of the best ways of getting rid of your own loneliness, and is a wonderful way to do what Jesus would do.

Keep in Touch . . . Wisely

Connect with anyone whom you assess to be genuine, and who is around you. But following your instincts about people can be important. Remember that being alone is better than being in bad company.

Some have found it helpful to join an online community. You have to figure out what's helpful and what isn't. I don't know how to say it better than: *Quantity of contact does not translate into quality of contact.*

I've had people tell me excitedly that they have more than 1,000 "friends" on their online "page." Is it a contest? Does the number of "friends" protect you from feelings of isolation and loneliness? We each have to find out what works best for us personally, don't we?

Some act as if they believe that quantity can substitute for a lack of genuine closeness. It is impossible to compensate for loneliness by filling our emptiness with a collection—however large—of superficial relationships. We don't need 1,000 people so much as we just need one person with whom there is mutual concern—that one special person who cares for us deeply.

Does it help you to be in touch with a lot of people through all the ways there are electronically? Is it more satisfying to be *with* people than just "in touch" with them? Do you ever find yourself communicating with a lot of strangers, and it actually contributes to your feelings of isolation and loneliness? Or does it lessen your loneliness to have people contacting you through a blog or in other ways—is it a good thing to reconnect with friends you haven't had contact with in a long time?

Some have said that the more time they spend on the Internet, the less time they spend actually having live conversations with other people. They say that some of the Internet connections can be or seem artificial. Do the electronic ways of communicating sometimes feel safer? Are they really safer? Are we ever trying to protect ourselves—to keep from being hurt? "If I get hurt, I'll just hit 'delete.'"

Can these methods of keeping in touch ever really take the place of sweet friendships where there is a face-to-face connecting between one human being and another?

Maybe by the time you read this chapter I'll have at least two blogs and will be tweeting and twitting or whatever, and spending endless hours in chat rooms. (Do they serve refreshments?)

Do Something Every Day That Scares You Half to Death

I am conscious that some of my occasional loneliness is because I get in a rut. Routine can be a good thing—making sure we get everything finished by establishing a pattern, a set way, some specific steps. But it can also cause and prolong loneliness when our world gets increasingly narrow. We do the same thing in the same way time after time, day after day.

I find that if I break some of my needless routine, life is more interesting. Drive a different way to work or church or to get your groceries or for visiting someone. Sit with someone different at a meeting or activity (unless you have children and other family members to sit with). Say hello to people you don't know (yet). Smile. Start a conversation with someone hunting for a good watermelon, waiting for the bus, standing in line at the post office, sitting in the doctor's office.

Let your children take over some of the household chores—now, there's something that might scare you half to death! "Roger, for one week you're in charge of seeing that Rover [that's a dog or a guinea pig or something] has a clean cage/habitat and food and water. Any questions?"

Start "small" if this is something that really IS going to

scare you half to death—do just one thing a day for a while, like smiling. Say to yourself, "Self, I have ONE SMILE to give away today. Just ONE. Who gets it?" Even looking around for that lucky person may bring you a whiff of joy, an inch less loneliness.

Shake things up! Don't just do more and more and more of less and less and less.

Be Willing to Make Needed Changes—Be Flexible

This is kind of like "Part Two" of doing something every day that scares you half to death.

Some who have studied common characteristics of those who are able to survive in situations where they are confined (often in solitary confinement) say that one common strategy is the ability to change strategies. People who survive are those flexible enough to make a change. When one thing isn't working, they're willing to try another. Is there a lesson in that for us? Do we try the same things over and over to overcome our loneliness, even though they're not working? If we're not able to be flexible, we may run out of options.

Become Involved in Service

For many of us, this is a wonderful way to bring ourselves out of loneliness. Don't bite off more than you can chew. Do what you can. This is something that can be very rewarding, whether you're doing some sweet act of service by yourself or involving yourself with groups of people.

Become a Volunteer

This is an aspect of service, but I decided to list it separately. You might become a "Pink Lady" at a local hospital, or become involved in some other kind of community service. There are so many who could benefit from sharing time with you. As we help others, we often end up helping ourselves as well.

My Uncle Chuck (Charles Franklin Middleton Jr.), ninety-one years old, recently won an award as Volunteer of the Year. He cares for his dear wife, Mary, who has Alzheimer's disease. He takes her with him everywhere, including when he does "Meals on Wheels" deliveries.

Find an Activity Where You'll Mingle with People

Involve yourself in things you'll enjoy, things that will make you happy and may also increase your chances of making friends. Find an activity where you can meet a lot of people. This can include many of the things mentioned in this chapter, such as walking your dog, joining a book club, or volunteering. It might surprise you what a difference this can make in your life.

Do something constructive. Remind yourself that sitting around and doing nothing will not make you feel better and will not improve your situation. Get out and do something you like to do! Here's a quick list of ideas to get your thinking started:

- Take a class at a local high school, college, library, or other community resource.
- Volunteer to help neighborhood groups.
- Join a gym or health club.
- Make some greeting cards and deliver or send them to others.
- Each day take a small step outside yourself to do something for another person.
- Join a book club, or organize one.
- Invite another family to come to a family home evening with you. (A braver version is to invite a family with young children.)
- Join the ward choir.
- Become a crossing guard.

Get Out of the House

Sometimes all it takes to get past our loneliness is to make the effort to socialize in some way rather than just staying home, staying alone. If you're homebound, you'll have to get out with someone's help. But if you can, DO get out of the house. If you can get past the inertia, you might be pleasantly surprised.

Let Time Take You Where You Need to Go

There are experiences of extreme loneliness where, after we've done all we can, we just have to let time take us from where we are to where we need and want to be.

Many years ago, I hit a depth of loneliness that I never thought I would experience personally. I had been encouraged to do something I didn't feel good about, and realized too late that they were wrong and I was right—I had made a huge mistake. I hadn't sinned. I hadn't done something that required repentance. But I had definitely made a huge error in judgment. I realized I had hurt others as well as myself, and that just added to my pain and absolute emptiness. I felt trapped, and I felt terrible.

It was during this time that I began to feel at least some small understanding of how someone might reach a point where they felt their only option was to go away—to leave. I remember looking at myself in the mirror and wishing I could disappear. It was an incredible thing to feel some compassion and understanding for people who had reached a point where they felt they couldn't continue living.

One day during this very dark time in my life I was looking out the window and noticed a little boy playing in a sandpile across the street. For some reason I had a vivid memory of having decided somewhere during my late teens and early twenties that I wanted to become as a child. And I realized that it had been a long, long time since I had tried to connect with that part of me—the child in me.

So I grabbed a spoon and a couple of toys and walked across the street. "Can I play?" I asked. He looked up at me with a skeptical glance and asked, "Do you know how?" I said I thought I did, and he let me sit down and join in. We made roads and bridges and lots of truck and digging sounds. I remembered everything! It was a moment in time that I'll never forget.

At some point in this hard period of my life, my mother, so in tune with my feelings no matter how far away I was, came to rescue me. She picked and packed me up, took me home, and helped me put the pieces back together. I learned SO much from this experience, including things about myself that I hadn't known, or hadn't been aware of.

This was an experience where I just had to let time go by until I was capable of "bucking up," getting up, getting out, getting back to doing and being. The sun goes down, but it WILL come up again. I know it's there, even on a cloudy day, and it seems to pick me up little by little as it rises and pushes away the darkness.

Seek Professional Help as Needed

If you have a persistent feeling of loneliness, please seek medical help. It might be a sign of depression. If you can't cope with your loneliness, professional help can be useful. For example, if you ever have feelings like "I wish I could die" or "I want to die," please get professional help. Find someone who shares your values and believes in the same basic truths you do, and let them help.

Attend the Temple as Often as You Can

Some people don't live very close to a temple. I know that. It makes those of us who do live close feel guilty when we don't go often. But go as often as you can—this is one of the places where I feel very safe, and I hope you will too. Even if you just go visit the beautiful grounds around a temple, do that if you can. Or sit in the foyer and just be there.

Do Family History Work

There are likely some of your ancestors who had times of loneliness. Connect with them. Find them and learn about them. Take them to the temple.

A friend shared the following: "As my time off began and I immersed myself in learning and research, I could scarcely find time to eat or sleep. I found a wonderful source for researching my German line and spent hours entering information into Personal Ancestral File and learning to use online genealogical resources. I found that, instead of feeling alone, I seemed at times to be surrounded by these ancestors who seemed so eager to be found, and I was definitely not lonely."

Read Scriptures and Hymns

I guess I don't need to say a lot about this one. I just know that for me, there can be great comfort and solace in times of loneliness to sing a hymn to myself, or just read the words, and to open the scriptures and read and think.

Receive a Priesthood Blessing

If I were listing things in order of importance, this one would be right up toward the top. Sometimes we hesitate receiving a priesthood blessing because we don't think we're miserable or sick enough, or we feel it's not good to overuse this privilege. Maybe we treat a priesthood blessing like an antibiotic—if you have too much or too many, the effectiveness may be affected. Not true! Anytime you feel like a blessing would help you, don't wait to seek one.

Pour Out Your Heart to Your Heavenly Father

Maybe I should introduce this final strategy with that oft-used phrase: "Last but NOT LEAST." Oh, this is FAR from "least." I hope you know that praying is something that can always help if we really do honestly and earnestly pour out our hearts to the One who knows us so well and loves us so perfectly. He understands EVERYTHING we are feeling, and likely weeps with us when we are desperately, painfully lonely. Let Him in! Let Him help!

There are times when neither things to look forward to nor friendship nor hymns nor other strategies will work. And perhaps the best idea for avoiding and assuaging loneliness is one we ought not to save just for times when nothing else will work. We need to turn to our Heavenly Father and the Savior earlier and more often. From Proverbs 3:5–6: "Trust in the Lord with all thine heart; and lean not unto thine own understanding. In all thy ways acknowledge him, and he shall direct thy paths."

I believe this deeply. Too often I do lean unto my own understanding (which is shallow and limited compared to His heavenly understanding), and I don't get very far in the right direction.

I've been thinking a lot about the difference prayer makes for me when I'm feeling lonely. How about this—when you have plenty of time and can perhaps turn off the phone, the TV, the radio, and anything else that might be a distraction (the children? . . . I realize that this is not going to be realistic for everyone), talk to Heavenly Father about yourself. Tell Him what's on your mind. You know He's aware, but tell Him anyway. Describe how hard it is to be lonely. He can help—and He will!

This is a long chapter and a very long list. How I hope you'll find at least one or two things that will be helpful as you search for ways to deal with your loneliness or to help someone else in theirs.

Chapter 3

The Gift of Friendship

*The person who tries to live alone will not succeed as a
human being. His heart withers if it does not answer another
heart. His mind shrinks away if he hears only the echoes
of his own thoughts and finds no other inspiration.*

Pearl S. Buck

Friendship—for both givers and receivers—is a gift. And it's
an incredible cure for loneliness!

I've often said that while others may gather spoons,
dolls, animal heads, rocks, bird feathers, or matchbooks, I
gather people. I don't say that in a sarcastic or silly way. I have
met so many incredible, wonderful people as I've wandered
around in my life. And I wish there were a way to keep in touch
with more of them. But it's hard to keep close to *everyone*, isn't
it? How sad I feel at having lost touch with some dear friends as
the years have gone by. I really mean it.

I always feel so bad when someone asks, "Do you remember
me?" Oh, I wish I did. I think I was born without a memory
chip. Is that possible—that someone like MEE could have
fewer than 2 gigs of memory?

However, I do remember clearly my very first friend. I was three years old when our family moved from California to Cedar City in southern Utah. Zonie lived across the street and up a few houses. We became friends the minute we met, and we've remained friends ever since then.

We did everything together, often along with other kids in the neighborhood—we walked to school, we played in the ditch, we collected movie star pictures, we slept out on her lawn, we read books, we dragged Main, we had New Year's Eve parties, we made popcorn on Sundays between Sunday School and sacrament meeting, we hopped on Mr. Munson's grocery wagon when it came down our street and bought goodies, we worked at Zion National Park. I had my Grasshopper Hospital on her front porch.

We even went on a trip to California on the train when we were just twelve years old—by ourselves! (Several mothers will probably faint when they read that.)

Zonie married Clayton, who lived down the street, and he became an anesthesiologist. They have lots of children and grandchildren, and even great-grandchildren, and have served missions all over the world, including several countries in Africa. And we are still friends!

What a blessing it is to have one or many friends! And what a shame that something so sweet as friendship seems so often to be ignored, to be declining. Maybe one of the reasons for the decline is that we don't value or seek friendship as we once did. In a world where many are experiencing increasing times of loneliness, of isolation, there is a great need for friendship.

I'd like to share two of my favorite dictionary definitions of friendship, both of which have sweet meanings. The first: "To be ready, willing, or cheerful, joyous—perhaps to frolick"!

How's that for painting a wonderful picture of the difference friendship can make for us! I want you to say to one of your good friends within the next few days, "Let's frolick!"

The other definition is equally wonderful: "An in-depth relationship combining trust, support, communication, loyalty, understanding, empathy, and closeness. One who has sufficient interest to serve another" (in Noah Webster, *American Dictionary of the English Language*, 1828, s.v. "friendship").

I also love this wonderful thought from Phillips Brooks: "We cannot tell the precise moment when friendship is formed. As in filling a vessel drop by drop, there is at last a drop which makes it run over, so in a series of kindnesses, there is at last one which makes the heart run over." Isn't that a great description?

Are there some words in these definitions that describe the kind of friendship you have, or have had, with another? I really hope so.

Friendship has been a source of joy and sweet companionship throughout the history of the world. We actually read quite a bit about it in the scriptures. I've been moved by the friendship the Savior had with His disciples, and particularly with Lazarus, Mary, and Martha. One of the greatest compliments He could pay was to call someone "friend."

The Gift of Friendship

I have always loved the story of David and Jonathan in the Old Testament. They truly loved and cared for each other: "The soul of Jonathan was knit with the soul of David, and Jonathan loved him as his own soul" (1 Samuel 18:1).

Naomi and her daughter-in-law Ruth had a wonderful friendship. You remember that they were both widows—both Naomi's husband and her son (Ruth's husband) had died, and Naomi decided to leave Moab and go home. She told her two daughters-in-law to return to their people, and Orpah did, but Ruth's response was: "Intreat me not to leave thee, or to return from following after thee: for whither thou goest, I will go; and where thou lodgest, I will lodge: thy people shall be my people, and thy God my God: Where thou diest, will I die, and there will I be buried: the Lord do so to me, and more also, if ought but death part thee and me" (Ruth 1:16–17).

How is your relationship with your daughters-in-law? How's your relationship with your mother-in-law? If she decided to leave Moab, would you go with her—to Blanding or Kanab or wherever she chose to go? Sorry . . . I couldn't resist.

I enjoy reading and rereading about Alma the Younger and the sons of King Mosiah—they went through so much together! They went on missions and were separated from each other for at least fourteen years, but were so happy to see each other again (see Alma 17:1–4).

There are many other historical friendships that I find incredible and beautiful: Heber C. Kimball and Brigham Young. John Adams with his wife, Abigail, and with Thomas

Jefferson (I still am amazed that they died on the same day: Independence Day, July 4, 1826). Helen Keller and Anne Sullivan, who were together for fifty years!

Think of the loneliness that might have been experienced without friendship—if Naomi had returned to her people alone, if David had not had Jonathan for companionship, if Helen Keller had not had Anne Sullivan (and vice versa). Lives have been blessed and saved through friendship.

Joseph Smith was reminded by the Lord that he had many friends who were standing by him with warm hearts and friendly hands at a time when he was suffering so much in Liberty Jail (Doctrine and Covenants 121:9). He taught that "friendship is one of the grand fundamental principles of 'Mormonism.' . . . Friendship is like Brother Turley in his blacksmith shop welding iron to iron; it unites the human family with its happy influence" (*History of the Church*, 5:517).

One of the best things for Joseph Smith was the friendship he found in his own family, including with his older brother, Hyrum. "In life they were not divided, and in death they were not separated!" (Doctrine and Covenants 135:3).

The Prophet Joseph knew from his own experience what a blessing and privilege it was to have a friend. He said: "Those who have not been enclosed in the walls of prison without cause or provocation, can have but little idea how sweet the voice of a friend is" (*Teachings of the Prophet Joseph Smith*, 134).

One of the saddest things about the Prophet's life for me is how many of his closest friends and associates turned against him. I can't imagine how painful and lonely it must have been for him to see those who had been by his side through extraordinary experiences let go and turn away.

President David O. McKay said that "next to a sense of kinship with God comes the helpfulness, encouragement, and inspiration of friends. Friendship is a sacred possession. . . . To live, laugh, love one's friends, and be loved by them is to bask in the sunshine of life" (in Conference Report, April 1940, 116).

And Leo Tolstoy pointed out the great need we have for friendship:

> I knew before that God gives life to men, and de-
> sires them to live; but now I know far more. I know that
> God does not desire men to live apart from each other,
> and therefore has not revealed to them what is needful
> for each of them to live by himself. He wishes them to
> live together, united, and therefore has revealed to them
> that they are needful to each other's happiness. I know
> now that people only seem to live when they care only
> for themselves, and that it is by love for others that they
> really live (*What Men Live By*, ch. 11).

So how do we make friends, or find friends? When I was a little girl, I found out that the Lombardi brothers were digging a hole to China. Their dig site was just a block from our home, and I got pretty excited thinking about the possibility of having a whole bunch of new friends from the other side of the world. Sometimes making friends is just a matter of being where people are, whether it's emerging from a hole dug to China or gathering for a fireside or attending a conference or volunteering at a soup kitchen.

Some of us can look in our own homes, in our own families, to find our dearest friends. I'm so thankful and happy for the wonderful friendship I have with my three sisters and four brothers and their families! It's fun knowing and loving thirty-one nieces and nephews, and watching them as their own children come along (close to 45 at last count).

It's a wonderful thing when nieces and nephews grow old enough to become friends. How I cherish these relationships!

My relationship with my parents deepened as I left home and began to write and receive letters. My dad wrote every single week that I was away from home. He expressed such sweet love and shared so much wisdom and good counsel.

My mother wrote as often as she could, and we became friends. She could tell that I was desperately lonely, especially on my first mission. She fasted for me once a week, sent packages as well as letters, and helped me feel close even though we were 10,000 miles apart.

I treasure my relationship with both my parents, and the ways in which our love for each other deepened even while I was so far away so many times. It's a blessing to have friendships in your own family.

But . . . even though I have a wonderful family and many good friends, there came a time in my life when I felt the need for a *close* friend, a "buddy," a confidante—someone I could pour out my heart to, trust completely, and be entirely comfortable with.

This was at a point in my life when I would be retiring from the Missionary Training Center, where I had been daily surrounded by wonderful people. I was also close to being "fired" (okay, it was really a release) from the general board of the Relief Society, and I knew that I wouldn't be seeing these dear friends on a regular basis anymore.

So I was praying to find a friend. I had always hoped that eventually my best friend would be a husband . . . but that hadn't happened. Hasn't happened (I correct myself). I hoped for someone who would get in touch more than a couple of times a year, someone who would want to know my heart and really understand me.

Then, on my fifty-fifth birthday, I met a new friend. I know this is a blessing, and I'm so thankful for Leanne and the great adventures we've had and the memories we've collected in the years since we met.

Have you ever heard yourself or someone else express the feeling that "If I could just find the right person, the right friendship or relationship, my loneliness would go away." They may be right. Studies show that a person with one close friend does better than someone who has several "acquaintances." It seems that the best situation is *quality* of friendship rather than *quantity* of friends.

Good, close friendships are so rewarding. Friends enrich our lives, enlarge our worlds, and give us a sense of belonging. They sustain us during adversity and rejoice with us when we're happy. In them and their friendship we find encouragement, comfort, and much to look forward to. "There is a friend that sticketh closer than a brother" (Proverbs 18:24).

Women especially serve as each others' therapists in an informal but often very effective way. We give each other emotional support and help each other handle stress better. We help each other make sense of what's happening in our lives. Meaningful relationships help us to weather difficulties better and increase our feelings of self-worth.

Really satisfying relationships take time to build and a lot of nurturing. Sometimes, however, I think we meet people with whom we would be very, very close friends if we just had a way to spend more time together, to keep more closely in touch. Some incredible people have come into my life for just "a few minutes," as it seems, and yet have had such an impact on me. I look forward to a time—maybe when we're in a place where we don't have to measure time anymore, and where apparently distance won't be a problem—when I can become much better acquainted with many, many people.

How can we find and keep good friends? Be friendly. That's how many friendships begin. Someone reaches out, is friendly, and another responds.

One thing I know is that if we don't make the effort to make friends, others may not reach out to us, either, and then loneliness seems to be perpetuated. It's a sad cycle that we need to get out of.

Don't wait for someone to come and be *your* friend. It's been my experience that the best way to find a friend is to search, and to *be* a friend. Open your heart . . . and your doors and your windows.

If you're looking for a friend, if you feel a need for friendship, try not to be too isolated or insulated. Don't lose opportunities for being *with* others by spending too much time in front of the TV or in meaningless reading or computer games or wandering online. Follow what Church leaders have encouraged us to do: Get involved in life! If you stay away from others, you may miss a sweet friendship that "could have been."

Remember that you are trying to make a place for yourself in another person's life. Do not think that just showing up will win you instant friends. It can be a long process, and most people you meet already have their own friends and lives.

Show a genuine interest in other people and they'll be more likely to show an interest in you. Take some risks in sharing yourself with others, in saying what's on your mind. When it works, it is worth all the investment!

Sometimes when we're lonely we may be too "hungry" for friendship, and we might scare people away from us. We might come across as so needy, so desperate, that others may feel they just don't have the time or energy to respond to the offer of friendship. When you find someone you feel could be a friend, try not to glom on so tightly that they feel suffocated. Let them know you're interested, but don't smother them.

We can be better friends by living the Golden Rule the best we can. We can keep confidences—never betray a trust. We can become better listeners.

Anyone can cultivate a kind, friendly, cheerful countenance. This reminds me of a story I heard about an Asian girl who was introducing her friend to her bishop. She said, in her broken English, "He not mean . . . he just look mean." What do others see when they look at us?

If you have friends to talk to, and yet you still feel lonely, you might stop and ask yourself why. Maybe the relationships you have aren't as fulfilling as you'd like them to be. Maybe you need to go out there and make some new friends who can satisfy the need for a deeper relationship. Or maybe you could take one of your present relationships to a deeper level. Something to think about.

Don't think that all your friends need to be near your same age, live close enough that you could ride your bike to visit them, or have the very same interests and talents as you do. They say that variety is the spice of life, and that rings true with rich and rewarding friendship.

I am enriched by my friendships with many who have entirely different interests and talents from my own. Early in my writing of this book I chatted with many who gave me ideas and encouragement. My friend Michael even offered to write a song for the book. And he volunteered some of our other friends to help! Wow! I asked him if I could at least mention his wonderful, comforting, healing song, "You're Not Alone," and he said sure. (There, I just mentioned it; I love that song. Sometimes, just to be silly, I sing, "You're not a clone!")

We probably all recognize that friends don't have to be

"clones." Even best friends have very distinct personalities. Age, gender, marital status, and shared interests influence the closeness of every friendship.

I remember my sister Susan going to play Scrabble with "Aunt Olive," a friend fifty-seven years older than she was who won every single game they played. How they loved each other!

I've made some good friends through visiting teaching. I still keep in touch with some of them even though we don't live close to each other anymore.

As the years go by and our lives are busy with family and work and all, even the sweetest of friendships can slip away. Just as flowers need water, healthy relationships need meaningful contact to sustain them. Bringing life back to an old friendship or building a new one can bring deep personal satisfaction. How about surprising someone (including yourself, perhaps) with a burst of genuine friendship?

Be forgiving. This can help both in finding friends and in keeping friends. I came across something Gandhi said that I find very profound: "I hold myself to be incapable of hating any being on earth. By a long course of prayerful discipline, I have ceased for over forty years to hate anybody. I know this is a big claim. Nevertheless, I make it in all humility."

Wow.

Is there anyone you can think of who needs to return to the circle of your friendship and love? Anyone you can forgive? What a wonderful thing that would be!

How about doing some crazy, off-the-wall things with your

friends once in a while? Memories are made of this, along with all the other things you share, many of which may be tender and difficult.

One of my good friends from my almost fifty years in Mapleton is Shirley. I lived just across the street from Ron and Shirley for almost thirty years, and I watched their family of eight children grow. Before I'd go to bed at night I would look out my window and check to make sure they were there, and that helped me to sleep better—I didn't feel so alone or lonely.

Shirley and I walked together. One of us would call the other and say, "Let's walk," and oh, we had such good visits. As we used to say (and some of you probably have too), "We've solved all the world's problems this morning."

Well, there came a time when some changes were coming in our town, and there was an empty building by the bank on Main Street. We came up with an idea of how to use it and actually presented it to the city. I regret to inform you that nothing came of it . . . but we still had a great time!

SHIRLEY'S GYM:
A PROPOSAL TO MAPLETON CITY

From Shirley Graves and Mary Ellen Edmunds

April 2005

Whereas the city of Mapleton is building a new building, and

Whereas that means there will be an empty building, and

Whereas there is a need for a women's gym,

We therefore and hereby propose to lease the soon-to-be-vacant building just south of Central Bank for

SHIRLEY'S GYM

SHIRLEY GRAVES—Proprietor, President, CEO, COO, CFO, Poster Child, Notary Public

MARY ELLEN EDMUNDS—Personal Trainer, Activity Director, Timer, CIAO, EIEIO

This promises to be a popular spot in Mapleton for the women of the town who are overwhelmed, overworked, overextended, overdue, overdone, and over the rainbow

EQUIPMENT AND AMENITIES

Recliners, TVs, old movie magazines and romance novels, snack bar, chocolate trophies, background music (soothing lullabies), fun-house mirrors which make one beautifuller

DUES

Membership is based upon bringing high-carb, low-chew treats to each session
Also, for each session, each member will please bring a blankie

DON'TS

This spelling is very close to DONUTS, and those who bring donuts will qualify for several "free" sessions

TERMS OF THE LEASE

For every pound lost by any member of Shirley's Gym, the company will donate $1.00 to the Mapleton Library and 40 cents to the refreshment fund for bridal showers for any relative of a regular member of Shirley's Gym

NOTICE

The windows will be tinted to protect those who are . . . uh . . . exercising

ANOTHER NOTICE

No dogs, cats, rubber snakes and spiders, or strong perfumes

FINE PRINT—PRIVACY NOTICE

If you are not interested in receiving ads about Shirley's Gym, please mail a note to Santa or the Tooth Fairy

OTHER INFO

There will be NO scales on site. Line of clothing to be designed by ELLYN (nothing smaller than 3 sizes too big). Details coming soon

EXTRA CLASSES will be offered in Plutos [this is spelled correctly; don't fret], 50 Ways to Fall Asleep, Napping While Sitting, Breathe Deeper and Live Longer, Very Slow Dancing

That's it. Shirley's Gym. An idea whose time has not yet come.

Think of someone who is a friend to you right now. What

makes him or her such a good friend? Are you safe with that person? Is there trust? Is there joy and pleasure in the friendship? Do you both laugh and cry together comfortably? Does that person make you want to live better and be better?

Elder Robert D. Hales recommended a good way to recognize a true friend: "Do you know how to recognize a true friend? A real friend loves us and protects us. . . . A true friend makes it easier for us to live the gospel by being around him [or her]" ("Aaronic Priesthood," 40).

And Elder Jeffrey R. Holland taught:

> We could remember that Christ called his disciples friends, and that friends are those who stand by us in times of loneliness or potential despair. We could remember a friend we need to contact or, better yet, a friend we need to make. In doing so we could remember that God often provides his blessings through the compassionate and timely response of another. For someone nearby we may be the means of heaven's answer to a very urgent prayer ("This Do in Remembrance of Me," 69).

Maybe I was born to help you at some moment or season of your life, and maybe you were born to help me.

Maybe you were born to be a positive influence on your children and grandchildren, or a neighbor, or a stranger, or anyone who might be hungry, thirsty, sick, naked, imprisoned . . .

As Elder Joseph B. Wirthlin said so beautifully:

The compassion of Christlike friends deeply touches and changes our lives. . . . Love is the very essence of the gospel of Christ. In this Church, prayers for help are often answered by the Lord through the simple, daily service of caring brothers and sisters. In the goodness of genuine friends, I have seen the reflected mercy of the Lord Himself. I have always been humbled by the knowledge that the Savior regards us as His friends when we choose to follow Him and keep His commandments ("Valued Companions," 32).

Don't ever forget that *you* have "friends in high places"!

We are loved so much by our Heavenly Father, the Savior, and the Holy Ghost—not to mention relatives and friends who are Over There! We may not know it, but oh, how *close* they are to us! Most of them you don't remember right now, but they'll never forget you or turn away from you.

Friendship: it's one of the greatest antidotes there could be to loneliness. So treasure the friendships you already enjoy. Reach out to form more, or deeper, friendships. And remember always how many heavenly friends you have.

Chapter 4

Reaching Out to Those Who Are Lonely

Rejoice with them that do rejoice,
and weep with them that weep.

Romans 12:15

With all the pondering and observing I've done on the topic of loneliness, I have felt an increasing desire to be more aware of others—more sensitive, more kind, more tender, more willing to reach out. I pray there will be an increase in our reaching out to those who are lonely. I pray we'll be more aware of the pain so many are experiencing, and that we will do what we can to reach out in love and compassion.

Be a friend! Loneliness is a terrible disease, but it's not contagious.

It's been an important learning experience for me to talk to people and find out about how much loneliness there is even with people who seem to be so happy and doing so well. I can't remember a single person I've talked to who has said he or she has never been lonely. And even if that *were* true for some people, they may not realize that there could be some loneliness just around the corner.

On Monday, February 12, 2001, I was in the basement trying to deal with "matter unorganized" when the phone rang. I answered down there in the basement, and it was my cousin Cliff calling from Maryland. I could tell immediately that it was bad news. My dear missionary companion and friend Mary Jane had died suddenly. I couldn't grasp that. It couldn't be true! Not MJ! Not Turtle! NO!

But it was true, and after I thanked Cliff and hung up, I fell to pieces. I walked around the basement calling her name and sobbing so hard I was unable to stop. I could not handle this grief! I was all alone.

When I was finally able to talk, I called my mother to tell her that dear Mary Jane was gone. We talked briefly and then hung up, and I continued sobbing and wandering around.

A few minutes later, I heard the doorbell ringing. I should have known—Mom, eighty-six years old at the time, had driven over to be with me. We sat and cried together for quite a while. She didn't try to say a lot; she just sat and cried with me. How did she know how lonely I felt, how hard this was for me? She knew. She just knew.

I'm sure I'm not the only one who has experienced, in the death of a loved one, a time of terrible, deep loneliness. You keep thinking of just one more thing you wanted to share, wanted to ask, wanted to say. You wish you had one more chance to say *thank you* and *I love you.*

I still feel so thankful that my mother reached out during this and many other times when she knew I was hurting and needed comfort. And I thank all the many, many others who have done the same through the years.

After our mother went Home in May of 2009, my brother Frank began calling me each morning, and this continues to be a source of comfort and joy. My brother John calls frequently as well. And my sister Charlotte and I have always called each other almost every day (when we've been closer than thousands of miles). All of us send e-mails to each other to keep in touch.

There was a wonderful public service message produced by the LDS Church years ago called *The Mailbox*. It shows a sweet old soul walking down her lane to the mailbox each day, hoping for a letter, but seldom getting anything.

A younger woman who runs each day and passes near the mailbox notices the newspaper and pauses to pick it up. She runs down the lane and tosses it on the woman's porch. Such a little thing . . . but it brightened the older woman's day and life. She had a connection with someone, however brief.

Have you ever had a feeling of when and how to reach out to someone who was lonely? One of my friends who lost her husband after they'd been married just a few years said that it helped her so much to have someone come by a while later and ask her to talk about her husband. She said that it really made a difference, and that it seemed most people were hesitant, maybe afraid they would say or do the wrong thing.

This probably happens a lot—someone is having a hard

time, and we're not sure what to say or do, so we don't say or do anything . . . and someone is even lonelier.

Kurt Vonnegut asked, "What should young people do with their lives today?" Then he answered his own question: "Many things, obviously. But the most daring thing is to create stable communities in which the terrible disease of loneliness can be cured."

Can you think of someone who seems lonely? Is there something you can do?

Can we offer a positive relationship to someone who is hungry and thirsty for attention and kindness, for someone to listen or just to be there?

Sometimes in trying to be helpful we may mistakenly minimize the sadness or loneliness of others. We may try to lift their spirits by saying, in effect, that "things aren't so bad." "Well, at least . . ." (and we tell them how lucky they are that they've only been lonely for a few weeks). Well, there went our chance to help, right?

Can we offer a gentle approach to those who may have trouble opening up and trusting? Can we be better listeners? Can we ask Heavenly Father what to say and how to respond?

Do you remember someone, maybe your mother, asking you, "Where does it hurt?" when you came in crying from falling down or whatever?

Sometimes we skip this step when we're trying to help someone who feels lonely and isolated. We move too quickly to trying to "solve it," or even trying to talk someone out of being lonely. I'm not saying that couldn't work in some circum-stances, but it feels like it might backfire—that it could make someone feel as if we weren't serious and didn't really have any intention of taking the time to understand and truly help.

It feels to me like we could avoid false comments such as "I know just how you feel," or "You're just like my cousin Stacey—she got really lonely once," or "Bummer!"

There may be times when we could ask, "Would it help if . . ." and then offer a few suggestions.

A popular ad a few years ago had a catchy jingle that in-cluded the lines, "Reach out, reach out and touch someone. Reach out, reach out and just say hi." Have you ever been down and out, almost unaware of the people and things around you, and someone smiled? Or said hello? Held a door open for you? Asked if you were okay? And didn't turn away when you said something like "Not really."

It can make such a difference to have someone reach out when things are "not really" okay in our lives. How lonely it is to have to bear such burdens without help! From my own expe-rience, for example, I think back to the night of November 7, 2000, when I returned home after having been gone for a week and discovered that my home had flooded. BAD flood. Whole house. Broken pipe upstairs.

I cannot ever adequately thank everyone who came to help—including those who showed up that very night. It still makes me feel emotional to think of those who helped so much in the months it took to put the home back together (after pretty much taking it apart). I felt overwhelmed by the kindness and generosity of family, friends, neighbors, and even people I didn't know.

During the months of renewal and restoration, when I was "cast out," I moved in to live with my mother, who lived alone, as I did. I think we both felt less lonely during that time we had together. I know it did wonders for me. We had time for just visiting—talking and sharing like we hadn't done in a long time. And I loved our prayers together each evening (even if it was always my turn; Mom felt unsure about praying out loud since she'd had a stroke a few years earlier).

That was a time when my aloneness was interrupted in an unusual, unexpected way. Has that happened to you?

Another, very different such time for me was in the spring of 1999, when I received a wonderful gift of "company" for several weeks. A beautiful pheasant, whom I named Philo, took up residence in my backyard. I soon discovered he had three wives! Yes, three. Wife Number One was Phoebe. She was the first one I noticed. Then came Phyllis and, last but not least, Phran.

You may think I'm nuts or pathetic, but I absolutely loved having those pheasants living in the yard and roaming around. I had such a good time watching them and telling our neighbors what was happening. "Philo chased Phyllis around the yard this morning." "Phoebe flew into one of my trees to get away from Philo." "Phran stayed in the yard next door, maybe to put a fence between her and Philo."

I really felt like Philo and his wives knew that I posed no danger to them—that I was, in fact, happy they had come to stay for a while.

I got so I recognized Philo's call and his wing-flapping ceremonies. He would spend a lot of time right below my bedroom window, and occasionally he even perched himself on the windowsill where I could observe him "up close and personal." Sometimes he was up before 6:00 A.M. At night he would sleep in the tree right outside my window.

This pheasant phamily (couldn't help that one) stayed for more than two months! When they left, I missed them so much. I watched for them for quite a while, wondering if they'd moved to a bigger place or something.

Maybe it was silly to feel so attached to a group of pheasants, but I can honestly say that I didn't feel so alone while they camped in my yard.

I won't stretch the story by saying that Heavenly Father had Philo choose my yard. On the other hand, I wouldn't put it past Him. He knows us so well and treats us with such tender care.

We're not pheasants, and we likely wouldn't think of going and camping out in someone's yard for a few months, but I know there are things we can do to cheer up those who feel alone. If we choose not to do anything, it's possible we may be moving away from joy, from sweet experiences, and closer to our own loneliness.

Ask someone if they'd like to walk with you all the way to

the mailboxes (if you have some of those "collection of mail-boxes" things in your neighborhood).

See if someone would like to go get a smoothie or a cookie with you. Or a surprise.

Plan a little treasure hunt for someone, sending them around the neighborhood, with perhaps a surprise lunch with a few of you at the end.

You could write some things on three-by-five cards (it's quite happifying if they're different colors, but plain or lined white ones work just as well) and ask someone who is strug-gling with loneliness to "pick a card, any card." You could have things written on them like: "Come to my place for breakfast tomorrow morning," "Find interesting shapes in the clouds," "Count taxis," "Dance and sing," "Go to the airport and watch planes come and go," "Take a walk on the beach." (this one could include searching for a beach), or even something like, "I'll pick you up Saturday morning, and let's go find some yard sales."

Let them pick a card randomly, or they could keep shuffling through the cards until they find something they'd like to do.

It may help a lot if you can find a way to give someone something to look forward to. "Would you like to go to a movie this weekend?" "Would you like to take a drive some afternoon and see the fall colors in the canyon? I'll fix a simple picnic." "Let's cruise around some evening and look at Christmas lights. We could give a prize for the ones we like best."

Encourage them to be honest in responding—something that we'd look forward to may be stressful to others.

It has helped me many times to try to imagine what it would be like to be in someone else's situation. "How would I feel if . . ." Heavenly Father looks on the heart, and I know He's willing to help us do that more often and more effectively.

Spend some time writing letters for folks in a care center who can no longer do that, or fixing their hair, listening to their stories, reading to them, or any other thing that might lift their spirits and brighten their day. Give time. Give laughter. Give friendship. Give yourself.

Deliver or send a card. Isn't it a great feeling when you find a card that seems to have just the right message for someone? Make a card!

Maybe you could take someone a plant or a little framed thought or some other little gift and say, "This reminded me of you," or, "This was calling your name," or, "This is a rent-to-own gift."

Once when I knew my sister Charlotte was homesick and lonely as she began her nurse's training at Ricks College, I had my classmates help me write her letters. I prepared all the envelopes, trying to make each one different and clever, and we ended up sending her seventeen letters. She said it made a *huge* difference. Hooray!

Could you take someone to an appointment? Could you take them shopping? Could you take them with you to the temple? Could you offer to pick them up for a ward or neighborhood social?

Have you ever had a time when you realized that in reaching out to help others you had also helped yourself? It's quite a magical thing, and it happens all the time.

We don't really reach out to others hoping for or expecting any reward, but it can't be helped—there are sweet rewards for being kind.

A dear aunt of mine who lived many miles from me in an assisted living center felt lonely much of the time. But some of my good friends came to her rescue. They brought tapes for her to listen to, baked cookies for her, brought their dogs to visit, and helped with her dog as needed. They took her to doctors' appointments and to the hospital, to lunch and to the beach. How my aunt looked forward to their visits! I can never thank them enough for their kindness—it helped me along with helping my aunt.

My aunt is Home now, and I'm looking forward to the time when there is a reunion between her and these friends of mine who generously shared time, love, and friendship.

Look around you during holiday seasons for people who might be lonely. Reach out to them. Include them. Enjoy them. Give them the comfort and assurance of being wanted.

I have a huge collection of memories of times when my parents reached out to others. This was not about "duty," it was about doing what came naturally—seeing someone in need and doing what they could. My parents were both genuine

Christians. They ministered to others in ways that were like the Good Samaritan. They were generous with their time, their compassion, their encouragement, their love.

I read years ago about a father who had a child leaving home—perhaps for a mission or a semester abroad or something—and he wrote her a bunch of letters that she could open as a need arose. How wonderful is that!

Children need love and attention. We don't have to go very far to find children who are weeping, neglected, frightened, sad, lonely, or even abused. Ouch! They yearn for happiness, a feeling of success, kindness, and a sense of belonging. Notice them. Talk to them. Nurture them. Share generously "the bright sunlight of love." What an incredible difference it can make for any of us as we receive a little personal attention, a little encouragement, a little praise.

I try never to pass by a lemonade stand without stopping. These are fun little adventures—the kids get so excited! Me too! I keep coins in my car for just such occasions.

When was the last time you invited someone over for lunch or dinner? When was the last time you sat somewhere different in a meeting because you had a feeling someone else needed to have company? Is there someone who is sitting alone? Is there anyone who is new in the ward? Is there a young single adult or a single mom or a visitor? Is there a child who sometimes or almost always comes to meetings alone?

When was the last time someone reached out to *you?* Our own experiences can help us to have empathy and to reach out to others. I have wondered if I would have been a better nurse—more sensitive, aware, and tender—if I'd had more experience as a patient. Eventually I did get a turn to be on the other end, to be a patient. But it didn't come until I was past forty (and past working as a nurse).

You know, offering compassion and comfort to those who are lonely is a way of keeping our baptismal covenant. President Harold B. Lee explained the blessings that can come from this kind of reaching out:

> You must be willing "to bear one another's burdens, that they may be light." You must be willing to mourn with those that mourn, and comfort those that stand in need of comfort. (Mosiah 18:8–9.) When a mother mourns in her loneliness for the return of a wayward daughter, you with compassion must forbid the casting of the first stone. It is the kind of mourning portrayed in the deep feelings of the marine on Saipan who wrote to us during the war when his buddy was killed. "As I lay in my foxhole that night I wept bitterly." Your mourning with the aged, the widow and the orphan should lead you to bring the succor they require. In a word, you must be as the publican and not as the Pharisee. "God be merciful to me a sinner." Your reward for doing is the blessedness of comfort for your own soul through a forgiveness of your own sins (*Decisions for Successful Living*, 58).

How about joining the "Secret Service" corps? You can do some kind things for people you think might need a lift, and if you want you can do them anonymously. This may cause the person who is lonely to suspect almost everyone of being responsible for a nice surprise, and it may even compel them to smile or say something to those in their neighborhood, their office, their church group, or their family.

Of course, it mattereth not if you do things out in the open. Sometimes that's a wonderful way to get acquainted and let others know they're not alone. And maybe you can enlist them to do something nice for someone else who also seems to be lonely.

President Gordon B. Hinckley talked about the importance of service—of reaching out—in overcoming loneliness. "I believe that for most of us the best medicine for loneliness is work, service in behalf of others" ("Women of the Church," 68).

I want to add a little bit more about homesickness and the loneliness that accompanies this very painful feeling. We know how difficult it is for many parents and others to see missionaries leave, but how about from the perspective of missionaries?

I worked with quite a few younger and senior missionaries during the forty years of my life that I was involved directly in missionary work. I met many who were terribly homesick, and I was surprised to know that they hadn't heard of the record I'd set in that category. I made this up, but I think it might be close to the truth, that I was as homesick as any missionary had ever been. I felt empathy for those who struggled with that.

I would always look for them on Wednesdays—the day new

missionaries arrived at the Missionary Training Center. I could tell you a lot of stories, but I'll use one or two as illustrations.

One Wednesday I found three sister missionaries sitting on a bench at around 5:30 P.M. They were waiting for interviews with their branch president, which would begin in about half an hour. I could tell—just by looking in their faces I could tell—that they were struggling a bit. I introduced myself and shook their hands. "Feels kind of weird, doesn't it," I said. One of them fought the tears. I said, "Hold on—I'll be right back."

I went and got my missionary journal from when I had been in that very place, back in September 1976 when it was still called the LTM—the Language Training Mission.

I came back to the three sisters and said, "Do you mind if I read to you what I wrote on my first night here?" They wanted to hear. There it was: "Edmunds . . . WHAT HAVE YOU DONE???" We all laughed, and we talked and talked. I hope it helped them even a little bit to know that they were not wicked or abnormal or anything.

I remember a young missionary who came to my office at the Missionary Training Center one day. His supervisor, knowing some of his struggles, told him to come and talk to me. As soon as he knew that I had also felt homesick as a missionary, he poured out his heart. He told me that some well-meaning person had declared to him that he was homesick because he had something he had not yet repented of! To me, that was a cruel thing to say. To discount someone's loneliness is one thing, but to call the person a sinner is quite another. Carefully and without screaming, I shared some thoughts and feelings, asked a lot of questions, and listened and listened and listened.

I had a painting of the Savior hanging in my office that had been painted for me by one of my brothers-in-law, a man who was paralyzed from the neck down, which condition I felt brought him very close to the Savior. When this young elder asked me, "Do you think I should go on my mission?" I looked over at this painting and said something like, "I am convinced He wants you to go and represent Him." We were both weeping. It was an amazingly sweet spiritual experience we shared—our understanding of loneliness, and our understanding that the Savior understood too.

He did go on his mission, and I kept the long note he wrote to me after he got there, thanking me for knowing at least a little bit about how he was feeling and why, and for giving him encouragement to continue his mission.

Write letters to missionaries. You can do it, even if they're not related to you—because they are, in fact; they're your sisters and brothers. If you've ever been away from home, you know that mail is like manna, and that a letter can make a big difference. Just write a friendly note and tell them you hope they're having a good experience.

Oh, if I—if we—could be kind and gentle with each other! If we could only hold back on all our "canned advice"! Does that make sense? I just mean we need to listen, to be kind, to do all we can to *understand*. Sometimes all I can say when someone pours out his or her loneliness of heart to me is to say with all *my* heart, "I'm so sorry."

Sure, I have "helpful" ideas come to mind, but I try not to just pounce on them. I'm not saying I'm really good at helping those who are lonely. I say stupid things; I do stupid things. But I try to do good things and say good things, and I know that can be felt. I know it makes a difference.

One of my own most difficult challenges with loneliness (and all the accompanying feelings) began on Tuesday, October 24, 2006. That was the day I moved from Mapleton to American Fork (both in Utah, around twenty-seven miles apart).

Originally my sister Charlotte and her husband would be with me to help—they had encouraged me to move so I would be close to them (just four doors away). But it turned out that just a month before the move, their eldest daughter gave birth to identical twin girls six weeks early, and the babies were both diagnosed with Down syndrome. So off went Charlotte and Art to Connecticut for a couple of months, and I was left to move by myself.

I have to say that I received incredible help from others—family members, neighbors, friends—but I'm referring to the actual day when most of the "big things" were to be moved from one home to the other.

I had looked through the Yellow Pages ("let your fingers do the walking") and found an ad that was very appealing. Things like "Rated #1 in customer satisfaction," "Let our family move yours," "Courteous and professionally trained personnel," "Modern moving with old-fashioned care," and so on. So I had called and made an appointment.

Three men arrived in a big truck, and I cheerfully greeted them, only to realize immediately that they were not friendly, cheerful men. Frankly, they frightened me. But I needed to move my things that day, as I had promised the family who would be moving in that they could begin by Halloween.

The day was a horrific nightmare. The first thing they did was demand $50 each for a "tip," and said I had to make an extra check for that rather than include it in the total cost. They kept saying I didn't look ready, and they sent me to the basement to pack things in big boxes while they started moving heavy things from the main floor.

I can't bear to go into detail about all the terrible things that happened; suffice it to say that at the end of the day many of my things were broken and many were actually stolen, including one of my credit cards! They used it twice at two different stations in the area around their Salt Lake headquarters. The police got involved and said that one of the three movers had many warrants out for his arrest. They had sent a felon—a criminal!—to move me.

This was one of the more traumatic experiences of my entire life, and as I spent that night alone in a "spoiled" new home, I was desperately lonely! I felt totally vulnerable. Every sound I heard was those men coming back—they knew where I lived, and they knew I was alone. I was absolutely terrified.

What did I learn? I learned that you should *never* move. Don't move!

Okay, I don't really mean that. But be sure you're not alone, and be sure you check out the movers very, very carefully before you hire anyone. Don't be suckered into something that looks too good to be true.

One of the most important things I learned is that there are some things you just have to let go of. I never did hear anything from the police or the moving company. I just had to let go. I realized after a few months that if I didn't do that it would "canker my soul" (see Doctrine and Covenants 56:16).

But one big reason I included this experience was because of something that happened the next evening, the evening after the Terrible Trauma. It may seem like a small thing—it may have seemed like a very small thing to the person who did it. But for me it made an inestimable difference. Someone reached out to me.

There was a knock at the door, and a neighbor whom I hadn't met yet stood there with a quart jar of homemade soup, still hot. She said she wanted to welcome me. I almost lost it, but I managed to hang on to my emotions until I had thanked her and she had left. Then I did lose it. Big time.

I hadn't located any dishes or utensils yet, so I just drank some soup right out of the jar, and it warmed my body and my soul. There is honestly no way to adequately describe what this did for me, the help and hope it gave to me.

My new neighbor had *no idea* what her kindness meant to

me. She helped a little buckaroo buck up! I had thanked her sincerely, but it wasn't until later that I explained a little bit about what had happened and how much I appreciated having her come that particular evening.

An update would be appropriate, lest you think I have lived in terror since that day. It isn't so. As with most hard, lonely experiences, this too has passed. I'm in a wonderful neighborhood, a fantastic ward, and I absolutely love my visiting teaching companion (her name is Charlotte, and we're very closely related).

Is there someone who has just moved into your neighborhood? Please help them to feel welcome—maybe they had the same moving company I did (they're nationwide), and they have had major trauma. But even if they haven't, there are so many things that are hard about moving. See if there's something you can do to help.

May we reach out to those who feel alone and lonely. May we do what we can for those who will "grab the hand of anybody kind enough to offer it."

Reaching out to others can be the best thing you ever do for yourself.

~ Chapter 5 ~

When All Else Fails,
Buck Up, Little Buckaroo

If there's sunshine in your heart,
You can send a shining ray
That will turn the night to day.
"You Can Make the Pathway Bright," *Hymns,* no. 228

You knew—you really knew—that eventually I would
jump off the track and start thinking of ridiculous ideas
for handling loneliness. Well . . . this is it. Please skip this
little chapter if you're not in the mood to read some of my sillier
ideas.

When you can think of absolutely nothing else, and when
time is not a factor (some of these things are going to take a lot
of time), see if any of these ideas would be "helpful."

Talk to Yourself

I talk to myself. I guess you can do that even when you
don't live alone, but I find there are times when it's nice to hear
a voice, even if it's just my own.

I have to be careful that I don't do this when others are

around. One day I was at the post office and I was chatting to myself *out loud* and suddenly realized I wasn't by myself. . . .

Sometimes I talk to myself about how I'm feeling: "Okay, you're lonely—what's going on?" There are times I can't find an answer, but often I can. "You've been up since 1:00 A.M." "You miss your mother." It's like part of me is talking to the rest of me.

Have a conversation with yourself and see what happens.

Make Up a New Holiday

Don't scoff at this one. You could be the reason for a whole new line of greeting cards! So give it some thought. Choose either a cause or a date first; it doesn't matter. We're not talking horse and cart or chicken and egg. We're talking New Holiday. What'll it be? What do you like? Do you like clouds? Then how about Cloud Appreciation Day. Do you think daffodils are pretty? Daffodil Day! Isn't that catchy!

Call and Surprise Someone

"I'll give you two minutes or twenty questions, whichever comes first, to guess who this is." Throw them off with a clue like "I was born in New Guinea." Then just let 'em take it from there.

Pretend You're Creating a GPS

That's an acronym with which you're probably pretty familiar if you've been outside your home much in the last five or ten years. I looked it up anyway to make sure I really knew what it stood for: Global Positioning System. I'm thinking it'll be safer if you create one for walkers rather than for drivers. It could get dangerous if you try to make one while you're driving. Glad I thought of that. I'm really not trying to write a dangerous book. Get a device where you can record your voice (and later duplicate the recording . . . friends and neighbors are going to want a copy!). Select an area of about a square mile, and go out and start making a GPS. You can even give it a clever name, like "Walk with MEE." Oh, that's really clever. Walk all around and through and find landmarks and signs and interesting things people can see when they get your GPS and go where you tell them.

Set Up a Lemonade Stand

Do you remember how? Or is this an adventure that you somehow missed when you were a child. Here's your chance. Yes, it will almost kill you to get out in public this way, but do your best. Make the lemonade, sure, but there are the extras that will ensure a lively hour or two (way to go if you last longer than that!). The sign: You need a sign that says "lemonade" so they won't think you're selling dandelions or fish bait—although you could sell more than one thing. The sign also needs to say how much you're charging: "25 cents a glass (or cup). 4 for a dollar." Be creative! Get some nice cups. Have change handy. Some kind of a uniform might be fun and draw attention to you along with the lemonade. Don't "freeze up" on me . . . remember that these are just stupid ideas. But oh, I'd love it if someone actually did this and let me know!

Write a Letter to Someone Who Won't Expect It

One of the easiest ways to do this is to respond to junk mail:

Dear Capital One:

You've been so good to correspond with me, and even though you always say the same things, you have made a friend here in [list the name of your city if you'd like, or make one up]. I could hardly believe how many different words you used on one rather small piece of paper. No wonder you had to make the printing so small—you had a lot you wanted to say, didn't you? You spelled my name right, and that impressed me. How did you know?

Dear Fei Furniture Mart:

I had no idea I was one of your valued customers. Where in the dickens is your store located, anyway? [And then you could go on to tell about your family, your recent trip to buy bread, and so on.]

Dear IRS:

I would like to cancel my subscription. Please remove my name from your mailing list at your earliest convenience.

Thanking you in advance, I remain . . .

(Hmmm. I'm thinking that one may not be such a good idea—you may be sent to a place where you'll be even lonelier than you are now!)

Dear Mrs. Higbee:

It wasn't easy to track you down, but I hope I finally got the right address. You taught me in third grade at West Elementary, and I don't think I ever thanked you for the time you took a few of us to your home for dinner and taught us about manners. My goodness, where did you learn so many manners? [Then you could tell Mrs. Higbee how well you've done since you left third grade—how much you improved in your class participation, penmanship, kindness during recess, and so on.]

Make a Happifying Calendar

This could be your personal calendar. Give yourself things to look forward to. Make them realistic at least some of the time. Put things on there that you'll need to plan for, like your ski trip to Las Vegas (it's kind of amazing the way strange things like this can pull you to the surface). What will you need to do to get there and have a great time? How about April in Paris? Will you go alone? How long will you stay? What are you going to see? Why not a trip to the Space Station, as long as we're dreaming of things that might not happen. Better pack a whole bunch of Dramamine!

Cook Something with Only What You Have on Hand

Perhaps it can be like a casserole. Choose a big baking thingie like a casserole dish. See what you have in your fridge or freezer, and try to select pretty colors to add to your dish. Cut it, stir it, add a little water or milk or both, put foil over the top (unless you love cleaning your oven, which—can you see the light bulb by my left ear?—just might provide another possible solution to your loneliness), mark it with a "T," and put it in the oven for . . . uh. DO NOT feed this to a baby! And maybe YOU shouldn't eat any of it either. If you still aren't feeling happy or better, let the concoction sit and cool for a couple of hours and then cut it in small pieces (about the size of a brick), wrap them in something, and freeze them. Now you're ready for company!

VARIATION # 7

This is connected, in a way, with the previous idea. This one includes finding a magazine or an ad with a picture of some beautiful food creation. The prettier and fancier, the better. Then create something as close as you can to what you see in the picture with just what you have on hand, from leftovers to a can of soup to week-old lettuce. See what you can do.

VARIATION # 52

Take the top half of one recipe and the bottom half of a different recipe and put them together and make it. Oh! You've GOT to take PICTURES!

Try Tying a Fly

That was sort of a clever title, wasn't it. I didn't work on it very long. Okay, let's get to work. Flies are not just annoying insects. They are works of art. Have you ever seen one? Go to a sporting goods store. (Cabela's is an example, but there may not be one within 500 miles of you, so choose another one.) Don't ask for directions. Just start walking around, looking at stuff. See if you can see some fishing poles sticking up—the flies and the kits to make them have got to be in that neighborhood. Select something that looks pretty and difficult. Try to make sure there is some message like "Everything you need to tie flies." Wouldn't it be a shame to get home and discover you were lacking an important something that was on sale right next to your fly kit. When you get home, go to work. Hey, this could open up a whole new hobby for you or even a cottage industry (or apartment or condo industry or something like that).

Create a Lost-and-Found in Your Home

Even if you live alone, as I do, you can create a wonderful "Lost and Found." You can have tangible things in there, like all the keys in the "Found" part of your space (but you no longer have any clue what the keys might have opened when they were younger . . . and why do you have five duplicates?).

Find Your Toy Box

What are some things you haven't done in a long, long time? See if your kids or some neighbors can take a break from video games, texting, and so on, and play marbles with you. Or jacks. Or jump-rope. Hopscotch. Hide-and-seek. Tag. Kick the can. Or, if you're like me and you can't run or climb anymore, how about Charades? Old Maid? Coloring?

Offer to Wash Windows for Someone

Take some equipment, like a bucket for water or a spray bottle or can of stuff, and some rags or paper towels, maybe a scraper dealie like some people use in their showers. And just show up at people's houses and say that you're offering a special on one window—the window of their choice—that for today only you'll clean it free of charge.

Put a Puzzle Together

Don't ask my brother to help you, though. He used to put a puzzle piece in his pocket so he could be the one to put the last piece in. It's a wonder he lived past the age of fifteen. But here's the idea—putting a puzzle together can be therapeutic. You're hunting for particular pieces—the edges, maybe, or the red that goes in the barn, or the blue in the sky, or the yellow in the sunflowers. There's a chance—maybe slim, but sometimes slim things can rescue us—that we'll be thinking while we're puzzling . . . puzzling while we're searching . . . and maybe our spirits will be lightened and brightened as the picture on the table begins to resemble the picture on the box top.

Creative Laundry Folding and More

Offer a prize for the child who can come up with the most creative way to fold a shirt (or some other item of clothing that can handle becoming a work of art). A ship? A hat? A critter? If you like to have everyone receive a prize, then make up some categories. Most beautiful. Most creative. Most unusual. Most difficult to guess. The more I'm thinking about this one, the more it feels like a dud. But there may be someone who will catch hold of this idea and have a wonderful time. Give yourself a free banana! And hey, that made me think of how much fun it would be to gather around your table (if you have one) and let everyone try their hand (with dull knives, or spoons, not anything too sharp) at carving something out of a banana. Can you even imagine how fun this could be! Set up a cleaning committee before you start this banana activity. CITRUS JUICE OR SODA POP WILL KEEP YOUR BANANAS FROM TURNING BROWN.

Write a Story

Make it as exciting and dramatic as you can. Be your own hero in the plot!

Be Creative with a Coconut

Do you know a place where you can buy a coconut? If so, and if this sounds exciting, go purchase one. Maybe two if you're feeling like having "company." Carve a face in it.

Send Someone on a Treasure Hunt

Oh, this could REALLY get you outside yourself. I'm not kidding. Once I sent one of my nursing classmates on a treasure hunt all over the BYU campus. Granted, back then it wasn't nearly as huge as it is now, but it was more than just the Maeser building, and I met a lot of interesting people as I went different places asking, "Can you keep a clue for me and only give it to the person who comes and asks for it?" Thinking back, I'm wondering if any of those helpers were tempted to just go to the next place themselves and end up with the prize. (I can't remember right now what the prize was, but I'm sure it was impressive and luxurious.) You could do it in your yard or neighborhood. Or in a park if you can make sure the clues wouldn't be hauled away by squirrels, dogs, birds, or curious children. You could do it in a house or a mall. And if you need to start with something extra comfortable, send YOURSELF on a treasure hunt. Hide all the clues and wait a few days until you've forgotten where they are and what the treasure is, and then hop to! Be sure to keep the initial clue in a place where you're sure to find it. Write a note on your bathroom mirror with magic marker (or a Sharpie, ha ha).

Go Whale Watching in the Nearest Irrigation Ditch

Okay, yes, this is very much like planning your ski trip to Las Vegas. I'm just trying to help distract you from your loneliness, and I've had fun imagining you planning what you need to take with you to the ditch. Something comfortable to sit on, even if it's just a blanket you can fold up ditchside. Something interesting to read if you think you can hear the whales and not have to watch constantly. (I'm laughing out loud just thinking about all of this; maybe it would help you be less lonely if you were to write a book!) You'll want binoculars so you can see the whales as closely as possible (yes, even in an irrigation ditch). Now, here's the extra benefit: Someone is eventually going to stop and ask, "What are you doing?" I want you to watch VERY CLOSELY as they react and respond when you say (without cracking a smile), "I'm whale watching." Oh, you've got to write down what happens!

Observe Ants

If you can't find any whales, maybe you could call some people in the area to see if they have ants, and let them know you're working on a project. This will be somewhat similar to whale watching, except that you don't have to find an irrigation ditch this time. You may want to bring along a magnifying glass instead of binoculars, but be VERY careful—if you look at the ants TOO long beneath the magnifying glass, you're liable to fry them to a crisp (and yes, I admit I've had some experience with this). Maybe you'll want to organize the ants into families, naming them or something. You could try to put little bits of color on them so you'll recognize them next time you see them. (As if!) Take a few notes. As you watch the ants, try to guess what they're going to do next. Try to imagine what they're thinking, and the conversations they're having with each other. Maybe the folks at Fei Furniture Mart or Capital One would like to hear about your ant watching.

Eat with Chopsticks for a Whole Day

Made of either wood or plastic, they're a challenge for most of us. This could turn into a great diet idea. Try eating peas or something. Don't do this if it frustrates you and makes you cry. Only do it if it turns out to make you smile or laugh . . . or throw peas at the wall.

Dig a Hole to China

I mentioned in the chapter on friendship that some boys in our town were digging a hole to China when I was a little girl. They didn't make it all the way, but maybe you will! One of your challenges might be where to start digging. You might live in an area where you'd have to go through asphalt, tile, concrete, or some other pretty tough stuff before you could actually start digging (after blasting). Maybe you could make a little sign: "Digging a hole to China; volunteers welcome." I think it would be prudent to purchase a book or CD of "Mandarin

Made Easy" so you can communicate with your new friends once you get your hole finished. Think of all the people you'll find when you break through in China!

Years ago, I read a story from Sandra Morse in the *Reader's Digest* about a boy in China who spoke to a couple of American tourists and told them that when he was little he had tried to dig a hole to the United States of America! Isn't that wonderful! See what could happen?

Read the Dictionary

This could be an old copy of Webster's, or one of those Oxford things where you have to use a magnifying glass (remember the one that had a little drawer thing in it for the magnifying glass?). Maybe you'll find a great dictionary online. See if you can reach a point where you can hardly wait to see what happens on the next page.

Study Words and Meanings

Find some really big words with lots of syllables, like *supercalifragilisticexpialidocious* or *accoutrements*. Look up the meanings so that you don't embarrass yourself if you plan to use them. See what happens when you use your big words in a casual conversation. Watch people's faces. Here are a few good words to get you started: *plethora, conviviality, ignominious, parsimonious, obstreperous*. (I admit I had to look up how to spell them and what they meant!) Eventually someone will call you a *sesquipedalian*, which means someone who uses big words, and that will break the ice, and you and that person just might become great friends!

Paint a Masterpiece

Every famous artist started somewhere. If this doesn't seem too expensive, go to a store that sells art things (let your fingers do the walking before you hunt all over town, unless that's something you'd enjoy—the excitement of the hunt). It would be good, I would think, to start with oils. Skip chalk and watercolors and go right to oils. You should be fine with just the primary colors—do you think? If you didn't go to Primary, ask one of the workers in the store to direct you to the primary colors. Maybe add one extra color just in case you need more variety. I think a small canvas would work for your first painting. Maybe you're planning to go outdoors to paint—where people can watch you and give suggestions and praise. So you might want some kind of stand to hold the canvas. Make sure it's one that will hold it STILL; it might be windy where you're going. What if you named your painting ahead of time (in case you forget during the process): "Borneo in March." "Flowers and Friends." "The Last Leaf before the Others Left." Something quite artsy and creative. And then, away you go, as they say. Oh, and if someone asks what it is, tell the person it's impressionistic or modern or a "lonely theme."

Paint a Mural on One of Your Walls

This is a bit of a variation on the "paint a masterpiece" idea. This time you're going to choose a wall in your home or apartment. (Caution: you may need to check with the landlord if you don't own your dwelling place.) Buy some paint and brushes. Ask the merchant if what you're buying will look good on walls. Maybe you can find a picture in a magazine or book that would look good on the designated wall. Try to include at least one animal (even if it's a caterpillar or a flea).

Memorize the Alphabet Backwards

Now, if you're so smart that you can do this in a few days, then put it to the tune—you know the tune I mean . . . the alphabet song. By the way, how come the letters are in that order? Is it because of the song?

Write Funny Thoughts on Envelopes

Here are some of my favorites to get you started.

- English major—YOU do the math.
- Don't make me use my librarian voice!
- Friends are God's way of apologizing for your relatives.
- If you're not going to learn from your mistakes, what's the use of making them?
- I had originally planned to entertain you by juggling

flaming bowling pins . . . but the rehearsals went poorly.

- If you love them, set them free. If they come back, set them on fire!
- The house was clean yesterday . . . sorry you missed it.
- Wisdom comes with age . . . sometimes age comes alone.
- Hard work must have killed *someone!*
- CARPE GOOGLE
- I've seen normal, and it ain't pretty.
- Organized people are just too lazy to look for things.
- Keep watching me—I might do a trick!
- If life is a journey, shouldn't you be moving along?
- If you don't like my cooking, lower your standards!
- If I can't take it with me, I'm not going.
- [On a snowy day:] There are snowmen falling all around us: Assembly required.
- What is the secret of refolding a map?
- Never try to teach a pig to sing. It wastes your time and annoys the pig.
- Good music is not as bad as it sounds.
- Ye shall know the truth, and the truth shall make you mad.
- Hush now, or I'll turn you back into a frog.
- Have you ever considered hibernation?

- [A sign for your office door:] The floggings will continue until morale improves.
- The only way to drive cattle fast is to go slow.
- [Another sign for your office door:] Friends welcome; relatives by appointment.
- God must love calories . . . He made so many!
- If God wanted me to touch my toes, He'd have put them on my knees!
- Thank you for not being pretty.
- I only have a kitchen because it came with the house.
- Housework can't kill you . . . but why take a chance?
- If you want breakfast in bed, sleep in the kitchen!
- Dust protects fine furniture.
- Joan of Arc was NOT Noah's wife.
- Ah, to have the complexion of an avocado . . .
- I'd turn back if I were you.
- If ignorance is bliss, why aren't more people happy?
- That's funny . . . I don't remember being absent-minded.
- I have multiple personalities, and nine of them like you.
- Ask me about my vow of silence.
- 24 hours in a day—24 cans of V-8 in a case— Coincidence? I don't think so!
- Truth aside, you look great!

- Paddle faster! I hear banjo music!
- I'm so far behind I thought I was first.
- Anyone who can swallow a pill at the drinking fountain deserves to get well.

Make a List of Things You'll Do When You're Not Lonely

One of my hopes for this book is that we can realize we don't need to spend the rest of our lives feeling lonely. It may seem at times that it's going to be that way, but fight that feeling, that myth! Write down things you're going to do when you are no longer lonely. If it helps, start writing things you'd do if you *weren't* lonely. Add to this list whenever an idea comes to mind. I pray you'll write down at least one thing, maybe more, that you decide to do NOW . . . while you still feel lonely. And maybe it will end up helping you diminish your feelings of loneliness!

I kind of suspected you would read this whole chapter, even though I told you not to if you weren't in the mood. I hope it's made you smile and even laugh.

~ Chapter 6 ~

What Can We Learn from Loneliness?

For I will be with thee, thy troubles to bless,
And sanctify to thee thy deepest distress.
"How Firm a Foundation," *Hymns,* no. 85

Loneliness can teach us important lessons. It can help us become more understanding and compassionate toward ourselves and others. The painful feeling known as loneliness can serve as a prompt to reconnect to others, including to our Heavenly Father.

I very much wanted to share *your* stories in this chapter; I would love to know what *you* have learned from your loneliness. But none of you submitted any. Hmmm . . . maybe I forgot to ask.

So I'll share one of my experiences. (Surprise!) This is another story from my short time in Africa, where Ann and I were sent to establish a health program for children.

I think that was a time of much loneliness because we were so isolated—separated from our families by more than just miles

100

and oceans. We were completely out of touch. We didn't have mail service for quite a while, and then it wasn't always reliable. We didn't have any phones in our area to be in touch with other missionaries, let alone our families back in America. Our living conditions were not what we were accustomed to, and I particularly had a hard time adjusting, even with the previous missionary experiences I'd had.

Part of my problem was that I was sick. I'd been sick on my other missions, but when my prayers about going to Africa were answered—"Yes, I want you to go"—I thought that meant I'd be WELL. I was wrong. It seems like I became sick almost immediately. And I was sick the whole time I was there. Asthma and allergies don't mix so well with hot, humid climates. There never was a day when I could breathe deeply and freely, or when I had enough energy to do even a fraction of what I needed and wanted to accomplish.

Have you ever been in a situation where you wanted to give all you had, and you ended up being able to give next to nothing because of limitations (health or otherwise)?

One day near Thanksgiving I wrote a short but revealing sentence in my journal: "Sometimes I really wonder if I'll ever in my whole life feel strong and healthy again."

Then came Tuesday, January 8, 1985. My incredible companion, Ann, who would literally save my life a few days later, had gone to another village with the couple missionaries. They were gone the whole day.

It was an unusual, unforgettable day for me. I had a long,

long talk with Heavenly Father. I cried a lot. I didn't want Him to think that I was complaining—that I was mad at Him or felt like He was the cause of everything I was going through. But I felt convinced that *He had asked me to come.* And I wondered why. What did this experience mean for me? What was I supposed to do with it and about it? What was I supposed to learn? Why was I having such a hard time dealing with my loneliness and despair?

This was one of the most sacred and important days of the whole experience. I was at a low ebb, but I wasn't bitter. If I'd been bitter or angry, what happened would not have occurred. I know that. I just needed to talk to Him. I needed Him to let me know that He knew where I was, and that HE knew why, even though I didn't. I needed to know some things that only He could tell me.

And so, on that day alone, I wasn't alone at all. I was closer to my Heavenly Father than I've been very many times in my life. I sat at the window of our place, holding onto the bars, and I wept. I asked, "What do You want from me?" That may sound like a sarcastic or biting question, but I asked it softly and humbly. I *knew* that He had not asked me to come to such a place for no reason. He doesn't do things like that.

I guess He knew that I had had a relatively trouble-free life, and that this time in Africa was indeed a "small moment." So He *could* have said such things, but He chose not to.

What He did whisper to me was so completely comforting and personal that the *feeling* remains with me today.

First, He put the following thought into my soul: "I will make it up to you." Those are my words, not His. I don't remember exactly what I "heard" inside of me, but that was what it meant in my earthling language: "I will make it up to you."

I told Him that was not what I wanted or needed, but He wouldn't take it back. It was a definite, strong impression and it wouldn't go away.

And then we had a long visit about what He wanted me to do. He asked if I had any idea of how much I would have learned and understood if I had felt completely healthy the whole time I was there. I told Him I likely would have missed *much*. He agreed.

He gave me an indication that some of my most important lessons might still be coming. I didn't ask Him how long He wanted me to stay there. It wasn't one of those times when I was in a hurry for *anything*. I wanted everything to go very slowly so that I could take it all in the best I could, and *remember*. I wanted to remember this very, very significant day and time in my life. I wanted to have it sink deep into my soul and be there forever.

I felt so personally and sweetly attended to during that time. It may be that there were others who helped to comfort and teach me on that unusual day (see Doctrine and Covenants 84:88).

I don't think I could ever do a very good job of sharing all that I felt on that day, but it was so sweet amidst all the awfulness that I let Him know I would go on and on if He asked me to—that I would stay as long as He wanted.

I learned lessons from the extreme loneliness I was feeling that will remain with me forever. I would not trade that particular day, and the other experiences when I felt so close to my Heavenly Father, for anything I can think of. And even though my lungs never quite recovered from their overseas adventures, I would not want to have missed those lessons, even with the price that was paid. I received and continue to receive so much more than I deserve.

I pray that I will never forget that day in Africa when He *visited me.*

I wish I could share *your* stories—that I could know something about your experiences and the things you have learned. I know you've had unforgettable times.

Can you think of some lessons you've learned from your loneliness? Have you become more sensitive to the feelings of others? Do you feel an increase in empathy and compassion?

Virtually everyone experiences loneliness at one time or another, sometimes very deeply, and if we can learn from these experiences, our lives will be richer and fuller.

One person who did share experiences that enriched my life was U.S. Air Force Captain Scott O'Grady. In his book, *Return with Honor,* he tells of ejecting out of his F-16 when it was hit by enemy fire over Bosnia in June 1995. He was twenty-nine years old at the time.

It took him a long time to float down in his parachute. He

was five miles up in the air, and he knew he was a "sitting duck" (or "floating duck"). But somehow, miraculously, he managed to evade capture! For almost a week, he subsisted on a diet of leaves and insects, drinking water that he wrung out of his socks. He had his radio with him, but he had to use it sparingly, because the enemy could find out his location just as his fellow Americans could. Can you imagine what a lonely, frightening time that would have been?

In a daring rescue on the morning of June 8, Captain O'Grady was picked up by marine helicopters. Later, he talked about what happened to him during that time.

> I underwent a rebirth. . . . Those six days in Bosnia became a religious retreat for me, a total spiritual renewal. I'm not recommending near-death experience for its own sake. It's a ride I wouldn't care to take again. But I will say that my time in Bosnia was completely positive—nothing bad has come out of it. From the instant that my plane blew up around me, I opened my heart to God's love. . . .
>
> By the end of [my experience] I realized that only three things mattered in this world: Number one was faith in God, the source of all goodness. Number two was the love of family and friends. That love wasn't something apart from faith, nor was it a by-product—it was faith's fullest expression. Number three was good health, the physical foundation for faith and love.
>
> . . . As I huddled in those woods, I didn't feel like Captain O'Grady, fighter pilot. I was just a scared guy

named Scott, getting by on his wits, discovering more about himself each day. . . . I am convinced that we are more than the sum of our material possessions, [and] that there is a life before this one and a life to follow. And that the point of our brief time on earth is to come to grips with what is eternal inside us—the part we'll take with us when we leave the rest behind (*Return with Honor*, 201–4).

Because of the way O'Grady described his response to his terrible situation, I'm wondering if Heavenly Father was whispering to him, "Be still . . . be still and know that I am God."

He could have given up. It would have been so easy to say, "I can't do this! I'm hungry! I'm thirsty! I'm lonely!" But he was learning some extremely important personal lessons. To me this is a powerful example of someone who was able to turn a very lonely experience into one that had a profound effect on his life.

If we were sitting together having a discussion and someone asked, "Can you think of anyone in the scriptures who was really lonely?" many of us might think of Moroni. Moroni had watched the destruction of everyone he knew. He was absolutely alone, except for the Lamanites, who were hunting for anyone who might still believe in Christ. I've read his description of this time repeatedly, trying to imagine what it was like for him:

> Behold I, Moroni, do finish the record of my father, Mormon. Behold, I have but few things to write, which things I have been commanded by my father.

And now it came to pass that after the great and tremendous battle at Cumorah, behold, the Nephites who had escaped into the country southward were hunted by the Lamanites, until they were all destroyed.

And my father also was killed by them, and I even remain alone to write the sad tale of the destruction of my people. But behold, they are gone, and I fulfil the commandment of my father. And whether they will slay me, I know not.

Therefore I will write and hide up the records in the earth; and whither I go it mattereth not.

Behold, my father hath made this record, and he hath written the intent thereof. And behold, I would write it also if I had room upon the plates, but I have not; and ore I have none, for I am alone. My father hath been slain in battle, and all my kinsfolk, and I have not friends nor whither to go; and how long the Lord will suffer that I may live I know not (Mormon 8:1–5).

It sounds like he's pretty sure he won't be around very long, doesn't it, and that he won't be adding much to the record. He knows he has neither room on the plates nor ore with which to make some new ones. He even gives a "last lecture," a final farewell, in Mormon 8:12–13.

But then he seems to wake up to the realization that his life's mission is not yet finished. There is work to be done. Moroni goes on to abridge the record of the Jaredites and write many of his own words in spite of his being alone.

Think of the loneliness of others about whom you've read.

How about young Joseph, whose own brothers sold him as a slave, and who spent many years in prison in Egypt.

John the Baptist spent time alone in the wilderness preparing for his mission, and later was imprisoned.

Peter was imprisoned, and God sent an angel to rescue him.

The prophet Ether had to flee for his life and live in a cave. He recorded on gold plates the final days of his people and the once-great Jaredite nation.

While the prophet Moses had his brother Aaron and others who were close to him, I can imagine he had times of loneliness during the many years he was subjected to the criticism, complaining, and disobedience of the children of Israel.

Many of those who served the Lord were called to be hungry, thirsty, naked, imprisoned, sick, and so forth.

There is so much about the Prophet Joseph Smith's life that indicates loneliness, and not just during the times when he was imprisoned. But I suppose his time in Liberty Jail is the experience that comes to mind most often—the time when he cried out to the Lord, "O God, where art thou? And where is the pavilion that covereth thy hiding place?" (Doctrine and Covenants 121:1).

Even with others in the jail with him, this period of more than four months must have been a time of deep, heavy loneliness and sorrow for the Prophet. And yet, think of the glorious revelations God gave to Joseph during this time, and during other times when he was in jail and in trouble.

There are many accounts of the pioneers who crossed the

plains, and there is so much of loneliness detailed in those journeys. I know I can't begin to know what it was like for them as they suffered in so many ways, including the grief of losing a father, a mother, a child.

Many who have been called to positions of leadership have spoken of the loneliness they have felt, and their struggles to feel worthy of their callings. President Gordon B. Hinckley expressed some feelings about this. For example, when he was serving as a counselor in the First Presidency, he said this:

> It is now almost three years since I was called by President Kimball to serve as a counselor in the First Presidency of the Church. During a substantial part of that period I have humbly tried to carry a great and awesome responsibility. I have known something of loneliness and worry and deep concern. I have prayed earnestly for direction and strength and guidance. I have called on these my beloved brethren of the Twelve. They have freely and generously given of support, assistance, and inspired counsel (*Teachings of Gordon B. Hinckley,* 671).

The following excerpt is from President Hinckley's remarks at a training meeting for General Authorities just a few weeks after the death of President Howard W. Hunter.

> I have received many expressions of friendship and brotherhood and support, and I have discovered, even to my surprise, that with all of this there is an interesting loneliness that comes with this office. That may sound

strange. It is strange. But it is real. One feels compelled to go to one's knees and plead with the Lord for direction and guidance, for strength and capacity (*Teachings of Gordon B. Hinckley*, 305).

And President Hinckley made the following comments during his first general conference as prophet and President of the Church: "Years ago I gave a talk on the loneliness of leadership. Now for the first time I realize the full import of that loneliness. I do not know why this mantle has fallen upon my shoulders. I suppose some of you may also wonder. But we are here" ("This Is the Work of the Master," 69).

It touches me to read of President Hinckley's feelings of being compelled to kneel and plead with the Lord. Perhaps this can be the greatest lesson—and benefit, if you will—of our loneliness: the realization that we need our Heavenly Father, and that of all the people or places or solutions we could choose to try to deal with our times of feeling alone and lonely, there is nothing more important or effective. No one understands better than He not just our loneliness but the causes and the cures.

We know that many other leaders, not just in the Church, have turned to our Heavenly Father for guidance in the midst of the loneliness of their leadership. Certainly George Washington did, and Abraham Lincoln, and we have accounts of many, many other great leaders who knew they did not have to be alone. I want to share an example from the life of President Lincoln.

General Daniel E. Sickles had learned that before the

portentous battle of Gettysburg, upon the result of which, perhaps, the fate of the nation hung, President Lincoln was apparently free from the oppressive care that frequently weighed him down. After it was all past, the general asked Lincoln how that was. He said:

> Well, I will tell you how it was. In the pinch of your campaign up there, when everybody seemed panic-stricken and nobody could tell what was going to happen, oppressed by the gravity of our affairs, I went to my room one day and locked the door and got down on my knees before Almighty God and prayed to him mightily for victory at Gettysburg. I told Him that this war was His, and our cause His cause, but we could not stand another Fredericksburg or Chancellorsville. Then and there I made a solemn vow to Almighty God that if He would stand by our boys at Gettysburg, I would stand by Him, and He did stand by you boys, and I will stand by Him. And after that, I don't know how it was, and I cannot explain it, soon a sweet comfort crept into my soul. The feeling came that God had taken the whole business into His own hands, and that things would go right at Gettysburg, and that is why I had no fears about you (John Wesley Hill, *Abraham Lincoln—Man of God*, 339–40).

I find this so inspiring! When we're lonely, weighed down with responsibility or worry or any troubling feelings, we can learn from our own experience as well as the experiences of others, that God is *always* available. *Always!*

One reason I'm sharing experiences of some rather well-known people is because of how they handled their loneliness. I think there are lessons for us that can make a difference when we're struggling with our own lonely times.

One person who always comes to my mind is Anne Frank. When she was still a young girl, she went into hiding with her family. In the face of extreme danger from the Nazis, and in the loneliness of spending twenty-five months in the isolation of a small, damp place called the Annex, she remained consistently cheerful and optimistic.

Many have read the book that came from her diary, in which she called the Annex an ideal place to hide in. Despite its idiosyncrasies, she concluded cheerfully that it may have been the most comfortable hiding place in Amsterdam, or even in the whole country of Holland.

Anne and her family were forced to remain completely still from 8:30 A.M. to 6:30 P.M. every single day for all of those twenty-five months (that's over two years!) so that no one outside the Annex would hear voices, or floorboards creaking, or any sound at all.

And even with this lack of freedom to move for up to ten hours each day, she still wrote in her diary that the Annex was "a little piece of blue heaven, surrounded by heavy black rain clouds" (*The Diary of a Young Girl*, 103).

Can we learn something from this young girl about hope, cheerfulness, and optimism?

When I had the unforgettable experience of visiting a

refugee camp in Thailand in July 1981, I found myself awed by the peacefulness of the people, even in the midst of their loneliness. Many were separated from loved ones, and they were wondering if other family members had survived, if they were in this camp or another, and if they would ever be together again.

Yet here they were, far from home and yet making the best of it. The evidence of their choices to be positive, kind, and cheerful did something to my heart that I hope I'll never lose.

Several times I've read Helen Keller's autobiographical account, *The Story of My Life,* and I feel so uplifted by her escape from the loneliness of not being able to see or hear. She was trapped inside herself, in darkness and silence, for five years. She later said, "I felt as if invisible hands were holding me, and I made frantic efforts to free myself."

And then something happened that changed everything, although not instantly. Through Dr. Alexander Graham Bell, Helen met Anne Sullivan. Helen wrote, "The most important day I remember in all my life is the one on which my teacher came to me."

Anne is just as impressive as Helen. She was "The Miracle Worker." She came to the Keller home when she was just twenty-one, and she stayed by Helen's side for fifty years!

Helen recorded that the last word she lost was the first she rediscovered: "water." She said, "That living word awakened my soul, gave it light, hope, joy, set it free!" Ultimately she learned to speak in several languages and graduated with honors from Radcliffe. She learned to hope, to trust, to love, to be very happy.

Listen to some of the things she recorded about what she believed (I found these all on the Internet), and see if even one of them can light a little spark in you and bring you a message you need.

I believe that no good shall be lost, and that all man has willed or hoped or dreamed of good shall exist forever.

Joy is the holy fire that keeps our purpose warm and our intelligence aglow. Work without joy shall be as nothing. Resolve to keep happy, and your joy and you shall form an invincible host against difficulties.

When one door of happiness closes, another opens; but often we look so long at the closed door that we do not see the one which has been opened for us.

Your success and happiness lie in you. External conditions are the accidents of life, its outer trappings. The great, enduring qualities are love and service.

I believe that love will finally establish the kingdom of God on earth, and that cornerstones of that kingdom will be liberty, truth, brotherhood, and service.

I believe that the welfare of each is bound up in the welfare of all.

Join the great company of those who make the barren places of life fruitful with kindness.

Keep your face to the sunshine and you cannot see the shadow.

We can learn so much from this great soul. Think what we would have missed if she had remained trapped in her loneliness, in her silent, dark world.

Maybe there's more inside of us than we can imagine. And maybe there are ways in which we can help others discover or rediscover hope, optimism, light, and life.

Loneliness is not all bad, or at least it doesn't have to be. It's usually just a brief trigger that lets us know we have to make some changes. Part of us needs to wake up.

Please look back in the chapter on strategies and see if you can find something—anything—that you can do to help relieve this loneliness, even if only a little bit. "Little by little" has done wonders in many situations. Think of the little engine that could: "I think I can, I think I can." Try something that has worked for you before, or try something you've never thought of doing.

Here's one more idea I'd like to suggest. Do some thinking—some pondering—about lessons you have learned from your experiences, especially the hard ones. Write them down. Do your best to capture what you've felt and what it has meant to you, the difference it has made. For me, there have been many lessons, and I want to remember what I have learned.

I want to remember that my Heavenly Father was always there. He cared about me during my difficult time in Africa, and He allowed me to have many wonderful, sweet, unforgettable experiences even with all the hard times.

Now that I look back after having been on the earth for more than seventy years, I have a strong feeling that I am tied to dear ones in many different places. It's as if I have felt a whisper that I'm NOT a stranger here—not in Taiwan, not in Hong Kong, not in the Philippines or Indonesia or Nigeria or anywhere else I have been.

My heart has felt comfortable and at home with people I couldn't even talk to, but with whom I have had sweet communication.

I've learned that the age of miracles has not passed.

I've learned that people everywhere are basically good and kind, especially when we reach out to become acquainted with them, to become friends.

I've learned that happiness is not in *things*, it is in *us*.

I've learned that hopelessness is a terrible thing, and that we can almost always do even a little something to share hope with others.

I've learned that different isn't necessarily wrong.

I've learned that it's a BIG world . . . and it's a SMALL world.

I've learned that no matter what God asks us to do, if we do our best with every single thing He asks of us, no matter how hard, He always, *always* makes it up to us . . . and then some. *Always*.

I've learned that we all need each other, and we're all connected to each other.

I want to remember how much I have learned about

Heavenly Father's love for ALL of His children—those I came to love so much too. Kuo Mei Hsiang, Ah Yee, Marta, Lina, Tibor, Brother Ocampo, Yoyo, Ibu Subowo, Aischa, Endang, Darsi, Cecilia, Broomstick, Blessing, the little girl in the pink shirt whose name I never knew . . . these and thousands more I've met during my life are ALL and EACH a child of God, just as I am.

We ARE brothers and sisters in a very literal and beautiful way. We're family! We learn so much when we're together. And, if we will open our hearts, we will also learn important things when we're all alone.

Who is our greatest example as we think about lessons from loneliness? Most of us will think of the Savior, and He is the One I've chosen to mention in conclusion.

Mother Teresa spoke of the Savior many times. Here is one example:

> When Christ said: "I was hungry and you fed me," he didn't mean only the hunger for bread and for food; he also meant the hunger to be loved. Jesus himself experienced this loneliness. He came amongst his own and his own received him not, and it hurt him then and it has kept on hurting him. The same hunger, the same loneliness, the same having no one to be accepted by and to be loved and wanted by. Every human being in that case resembles Christ in his loneliness; and that is the hardest part, that's real hunger (*A Gift for God*, 30–31).

I particularly think of His loneliness during His final hours on this earth. He was neither welcomed nor wanted by His own.

Here is the One who would heal our loneliness—who would take upon Himself ALL our heavy burdens, all our sins and our suffering, our agony and pain—and He felt everything that we would feel. Maybe it still hurts Him in some way when we don't respond to what He has made possible for us, when we don't turn to Him for comfort, for understanding, for healing.

There have been some beautiful, tender messages shared about the Savior and His journey to save us, to make Heavenly Father's plan a genuine plan of happiness. One of those that touched me very, very deeply was Elder Jeffrey R. Holland's message during the 2009 April general conference. He said:

> My Easter-season message today is intended for everyone, but it is directed in a special way to those who are alone or feel alone or, worse yet, feel abandoned. These might include those longing to be married, those who have lost a spouse, and those who have lost—or have never been blessed with—children. Our empathy embraces wives forsaken by their husbands, husbands whose wives have walked away, and children bereft of one or the other of their parents—or both. This group can find within its broad circumference a soldier far from home, a missionary in those first weeks of homesickness, or a father out of work, afraid the fear in his eyes will be visible to his family. In short it can include all of us at various times in our lives.

To all such, I speak of the loneliest journey ever made and the unending blessings it brought to all in the human family. I speak of the Savior's solitary task of shouldering alone the burden of our salvation. Rightly He would say: "I have trodden the winepress alone; and of the people there was none with me: . . . I looked, and there was none to help; and I wondered that there was none to uphold [me]" (Isaiah 63:3, 5; see also D&C 76:107; 88:106; 133:50) ("None Were with Him," 86–88).

Jesus Christ triumphed over death, and He also triumphed over loneliness. As He hung on the cross and felt His Father's withdrawal, He cried out, but He finished what He had been sent to accomplish. He is truly our Savior and Redeemer, with healing in His wings, and a perfectly understanding heart. He healed our loneliness as well as His. Come unto Him!

Chapter 7

The Blessing of Solitude

He answers privately,
Reaches my reaching.
"Where Can I Turn for Peace," *Hymns,* no. 129

When I was much younger, we had a chorister who used to really "pump us up" during the singing of "Master, the Tempest Is Raging" (*Hymns,* no. 105). It says in the hymnbook that it's supposed to be sung fervently, and we really did sing it that way!

Master, the tempest is raging!
The billows are tossing high!
The sky is o'ershadowed with blackness.
No shelter or help is nigh.
Carest thou not that we perish?
How canst thou lie asleep
When each moment so madly is threat'ning
A grave in the angry deep?

I'm going to admit that as we sang louder—and it seemed like we sang faster, too—I'd get pretty nervous. Tempest is raging . . . billows (whatever they were; I figured only ship captains and pirates really knew) tossing high . . . blackness . . . no shelter, no help . . . we're going to perish! . . . I'm headed for a grave in the angry deep!

Then we'd get to the last part of the chorus. Oh, thank goodness for the chorus! *Peace, be still.* We would sing it a little softer than the other words.

I used to wait for that line through all the rest of the song: the storm-tossed sea, demons, waters swallowing ships . . . all of it. Because I knew that eventually He would get up and tell them all to stop.

"Peace, be still." Isn't that a beautiful phrase?

Our Heavenly Father and the Savior ask us to be still. Think about scriptures like these: "Let your hearts be comforted concerning Zion; for all flesh is in mine hands; be still and know that I am God" (Doctrine and Covenants 101:16). "Be still, and know that I am God: I will be exalted among the heathen, I will be exalted in the earth" (Psalm 46:10).

Why do you think They ask this of us? What do you think They mean?

Do we listen better when we're still? Is that why and how we come to know that He is God?

Our trials, our sorrow, our adversity can almost compel us to reach for understanding, to search our souls to find meaning for our experiences, to find the place where we can "be still and know" that God IS God, He is in His heaven, and He is aware of us and wants to talk to us about all we are feeling and thinking.

Maybe when God is asking us to "be still and know" that He is God, He understands that distractions, even pleasant ones, can make it hard for us to hear Him. With music playing, people talking, TVs blaring, and so on, we can't be truly STILL . . . and when we're still, we hear better, and we listen more carefully. And that's when God can remind us that He is there, and how much we need Him.

I get lots of great ideas when I'm being still, and I often say things like, "Oh, thank You! That's a wonderful idea!" I know where those ideas come from.

How is solitude different from loneliness? To me, there is a world of difference. They may look or seem alike from the outside, but what happens on the inside, in our soul, our center, is very different. The resemblance between the two disappears the instant we go inside.

As I see it, words like *lonesome* and *lonely* describe the pain of being alone when we don't want to be, and *solitude* describes the joy of being alone as a choice, a need. Loneliness depletes our bodies and minds; solitude can restore them. Loneliness can feel like we're being punished or abandoned; solitude can be something we cherish.

There are words that help describe solitude, and some of the words may even be considered synonyms: *contemplation, meditation, pondering, considering, renewal, enrichment, silence, quietness, calmness, refreshment.* What beautiful words.

Choosing to be alone is not the same thing as being lonely. The difference is perhaps like the difference between rowing and drifting. It's important to take time sometimes to make sure we're headed in a purposeful direction. Thoughtful "alone time" can help us make some course corrections as needed, refine our priorities, get a clearer sense of direction. Solitude can give us the chance to regain perspective. It renews us for the challenges we face. It allows us to get back into the position of being in charge of our own lives rather than being driven by schedules, lists, and demands from without.

I know people who say that their choice to be alone provides them with wonderful, satisfying company. Isn't that great? Sometimes I feel that's true with me, but I know I'm not skilled at it—I'm still gaining experience.

I first became aware of solitude—although I didn't know what to call it—when I was a teenager. We had moved to Mapleton, Utah, and ours was the very last house on the road. I would take our boxer dog, Genny, and we'd walk up the road to the foothills in the early evening. She would stand guard while I'd sit and pray and then just think. I always came away from those experiences refreshed and renewed.

Solitude is a way to nurture and commune with our own souls. For me, it's like I have a chance to ask myself, "How are you doing?" It's an opportunity for digging deep—for thinking more deliberately and deeply than I usually do. The philosopher Martin Buber said that "solitude is the place of purification."

I've discovered a comforting and helpful thing: Loneliness can be turned to solitude. I've learned this for myself, and I've had many others confirm the feeling. We can actually discover and enjoy a retreat from our busy, sometimes noisy lives, and a chance for spiritual renewal.

I know there are times when I try to "cure" my loneliness by jumping into a frenzy of busy-ness. This might help a little bit initially, but in the long run it doesn't really work. It's hard to find solitude while watching TV, attending a sporting event, going to a movie, or other such things.

One thing that happens to me when I work to turn my loneliness into solitude is that I no longer feel alone. I feel closer to God, and I even feel closer to myself, if that makes sense. Lord Byron described it this way: "in solitude, when we are least alone."

I think solitude—meditation, pondering, contemplation, and all—is something we can get better at, something we can cultivate. Our meditation, our reflection, can become increasingly rewarding and emotionally refreshing.

It can start with just trying to listen to our Heavenly Father as well as He listens to us. He's never not listening! He's never not paying attention! He's never not watching over us kindly and carefully! I am convinced this is true.

I'm able to look at myself in a more objective way during solitude than is usually possible. It brings so much self-awareness! It gives me the feeling of being loved and cared for by sources other than fellow earthlings. It reminds me of who I am—a child of God—and brings sweet solace.

My solitude consists of more counseling with my Heavenly Father than I do at other times. Alma Junior recommended this to his son Helaman—that he counsel with the Lord (see Alma 37:37).

Is it possible that we can turn our thoughts to a loving Heavenly Father more readily and consistently, not just when we're lonely, but in a manner so that when we ARE lonely, we can feel Him close to us? We can draw sustenance for our spirit, for our soul, from the quiet and privacy of solitude. Sweet re-freshment. Replenishment. Peacefulness.

Although the scriptures tell us very little about the Savior's personal life, we know that He sought and enjoyed solitude. He looked for opportunities for meditation, prayer, stillness. He seemed to find in His solitude a renewing, a chance to be close to His Father, to counsel with Him, to be instructed and strengthened and comforted.

Joseph Smith knelt in solitude to ask a question of God. I'm convinced that this need for solitude is evident in the lives of all prophets and many, many others.

One person I love to learn about and can hardly wait to meet someday is Heber C. Kimball. He is described by Orson F. Whitney as a man who loved solitude: "Heber's temperament was religious and poetical. Sociable as he was, and even bub-bling over with mirth, at times, his soul was essentially of a solemn cast. He loved solitude, not with the selfish spirit of the misanthrope, but for the opportunities it gave of communing with his own thoughts—a pleasure that only poet minds truly feel—and of listening to the voice of God and nature, expressed in all the countless and varied forms of life" (*Life of Heber C. Kimball*, 13).

Contrast these examples with the attempts of the adversary to distract us, to keep us from seeking solitude. Maybe he doesn't want us to experience solitude! Maybe he hates it! He'd rather have us be noisy, busy, occupied—distracted.

Elder Neal A. Maxwell put it this way: "Evil always seeks company, for it cannot be by itself alone. Satan detests solitude, for solitude turns him in upon himself, reminding him of what glories might have been" (*Of One Heart*, 50).

A verse from King Benjamin's address helps describe at least one aspect of solitude. This is one of my 1,000 favorite verses of scripture:

> And moreover, I would desire that ye should consider on the blessed and happy state of those that keep the commandments of God. For behold, they are blessed in all things, both temporal and spiritual; and if they hold out faithful to the end they are received into heaven, that thereby they may dwell with God in a state of neverending happiness. O remember, remember that these things are true; for the Lord God hath spoken it (Mosiah 2:41).

What is King Benjamin asking us to do? He's asking us to

consider! And how can we consider if we don't take some time to do so?

What can we learn and feel if we *consider* on the blessed and happy state of those that keep the commandments of God? Is it possible that we could remember that obedience brings happiness? And that it also brings blessings both temporal and spiritual?

Can we consider what it means to endure—to hold out faithful to the end—and what it will mean to be received into heaven to dwell with God in a state of never-ending happiness? Oh! this gives me so many happifying feelings—so much to *consider,* to think about, to ponder!

And of course I am struck with the way King Benjamin finishes this verse and chapter—asking us to *remember* (and saying it twice), and reminding us that he is speaking for the Lord God. These are not just his words.

During busy times in our lives, when it's hard to carve out time for solitude, we still could have an amazing time with even one verse of scripture such as the one I've just shared. We could be "considering" off and on as we ride a bus, walk to a class, bathe a baby, hunt for deer, wait for a fish to bite, wash the dishes (some of us still do that), watch a sunset, wait for an appointment, wait for the aspirin to work, fly a kite, distribute newspapers, hike the highest mountain. . . . But technology sometimes seems to crowd out our chances for meditation and contemplation, for soul searches and stillness. Have you noticed that too?

I can tell when it's been a while since I've pondered, since I've been alone with my thoughts. It's like they're calling to me. "We need some time. We need some attention. Remember how you said you'd get back to us? Did you have some idea of *when?*"

Emma Lou Thayne speaks of the years "when I felt totally accompanied with five little people. From room to room and wall to wall, even in the bathroom. What mother doesn't know the story? Silence and solitude were never mine. Unless I stayed up all night one night a week, which I did. Or I worked on my writing and projects between 11 P.M. and 3 A.M. when the rest of the house was quiet" ("Learning Is Nurture," 103).

In her refreshing, thought-provoking book, *The Holiness of Everyday Life,* Joan B. MacDonald speaks of the importance of finding space and time for solitude:

> We all need time to be alone with ourselves, to rest from the business of our days, to separate from others and reconnect with the reality of God. From experiences in quiet, introspective times, times with the scriptures, or times of prayer, we get back in touch with the central truth of who we are in a way that goes beyond definition or description in words. We reach out to touch God, he touches us, and we find our selfhood nurtured and affirmed (*The Holiness of Everyday Life,* 43).

Many people actively seek the chance to spend hours or days by themselves collecting their thoughts (isn't that a fun description to think about?), making decisions, remembering, or just relaxing, and they don't feel lonely.

Even when life is good and full, challenging and rewarding, there are times when we must be alone, be still. Everyone
needs these times for spiritual refreshment and renewal—time
to be quiet, to be silent. There are things only the soul can hear
clearly and plainly.

Our Heavenly Father instructs us to ask, to seek, to knock.
And times of solitude seem like ideal times to do that—to do
our asking, our seeking, our knocking. "Then shall ye call upon
me, and ye shall go and pray unto me, and I will hearken unto
you. And ye shall seek me, and find me, when ye shall search
for me with all your heart. And I will be found of you, saith the
Lord" (Jeremiah 29:12–14).

President Spencer W. Kimball tied prayer to solitude:
"Solitude is rich and profitable. When we pray alone with God,
we shed all sham and pretense, all hypocrisy and arrogance.
. . . In solitude we, too, may pray with greater depth and fervor"
(*Faith Precedes the Miracle*, 209).

Have you ever met anyone who seems afraid to be alone?
Maybe afraid to let the thoughts and feelings inside his or her
soul come to the surface?

Elouise Bell shared some feelings about the difficulty of
finding solitude that acknowledge the challenges some may
experience:

> There are many reasons: there's too much to do; I
> have too many responsibilities; there's not enough time;
> there's no convenient place to enjoy solitude; I can't sit
> down and do nothing while the list of today's duties nags

at my conscience. You can add to the list, I know. There are cultural reasons for our avoidance of stillness and solitude as well: our western culture (as contrasted with the culture of the Far East) doesn't value reflection and meditation; we have long confused stillness with idleness, and we view idleness as of the devil; our culture particularly discourages women from idleness, reflection, and so forth. All these assessments are true, but there is a deeper reason why I, for one, have a problem with stillness. I think many share it. The great English dictionarymaker, writer, and speaker Samuel Johnson shared my weakness. "It may be laid down," he said, "that when a man cannot bear his own company there is something wrong. He must fly from himself, either because he feels a tediousness in life from . . . an empty mind, . . . or he must be afraid of the intrusion of some unpleasing ideas, and, perhaps, is struggling to escape from the remembrance of a loss, the fear of a calamity, or some other thought of greater horror" ("Peace, Be Still," 21).

Being alone does bother some people. I know that. They don't seem to easily feel the comfort, peace, and calm that others do.

If the thought of being alone frightens you or bothers you, maybe you could start little by little. Mothers with children speak of their time in the shower being their solitude. Some have even said it's while they're folding clothes that they can be "alone."

I know there are some seasons where it's much more difficult to find or create stillness and solitude. Maybe that's when we are more aware of and thankful for personal prayer, for some stillness during the time we partake of the sacrament, during our chances to be in a temple, or on a walk . . . or in the shower.

Is it possible that creating even a small oasis of solitude in a wildly busy day can bring an increase in our ability to better handle the wild and busy?

Some people do feel they are way too busy for time alone, for solitude. And others don't seem to know what to do with their "alone time." I've had people tell me that they get feeling so bored! As someone who does not get bored, and can't remember ever being bored, I wish there were a system in which those for whom time drags could give some of their minutes and hours to those of us for whom time scoots along at speeds that pretty much take our breath away.

Much of my solitude comes in the early-morning hours. I know I've mentioned in writing and in speaking ad nauseum about how early I get up (usually), and how I love those hours before everyone and everything else is awake.

I seem to live in a different time zone. Because I live alone, I can usually go to bed whenever I get tired, and that often happens around five or six P.M. I read for a while, maybe work on a puzzle or two, and then my mind is "settled" and I am usually asleep between six and seven o'clock.

So I get up early. Maybe I was supposed to be born in Sweden or something—although I have to say that this hasn't always been my schedule of choice. I used to be a "night owl," and I found it hard to get up early for a morning shift at the hospital or an early class at school.

But that has all changed, and, in the words of youth, "I'm, like, TOTALLY a morning person!" I'm usually up by two or three A.M. I absolutely love those early-morning hours! I get so much done. My mind seems clear and responsive.

But not everyone lives alone, as I do, with the freedom to be an "early to bed and early to rise" person. By the way, I need to get something off my chest about this: Whoever said that going to bed early and rising early makes a man [or woman] "healthy, wealthy, and wise" just put those words in because they fit and rhymed. I'm not all that healthy, less wealthy, and not very wise . . . but I'm content, mostly happy, and thankful for an abundance of incredible blessings.

That's another thing solitude provides for me—the chance to express deep appreciation for so many blessings. In times of stillness I can be specific. I can actually count my many blessings, and, yes, name them one by one. And of course it does indeed surprise me what Heavenly Father has done!

And I do love the blessing of early mornings. Elder Neal A. Maxwell shared this: "Divine guidance is so crucial . . . that we need to go out of our way to put ourselves in a situation in which such special help can be given. President David O. McKay spoke of how the morning hours, before we are cluttered with the cares of day, are especially conducive to inspiration. Others have felt that solitude and reading the scriptures can create an atmosphere conducive to the Spirit and can be developed" (*Wherefore, Ye Must Press Forward*, 121).

And I can't resist adding another one from him, because he put things so well! "We rest and have some solitude in order to better serve those who may contribute to our fatigue!" (*We Will Prove Them Herewith*, 121).

I read somewhere that a Hindu man was asked how he was able to maintain the great serenity and peace he had about him, no matter what pressures he faced. His answer: "I never leave my place of meditation." Every morning he meditated for thirty minutes. Then he never left that place in his mind—he maintained the spirit of that place throughout the day amid his pressures.

I'm thinking that if we have a strong desire for solitude, and if we ask Heavenly Father to help us, we'll find a creative way to have even a few minutes for quiet meditation.

Two of my brothers spend time riding their bikes up Provo Canyon together or alone, and that's a time of sweet solitude for them.

When I was younger I did a lot of ironing, and it was a time for thinking. I had no idea then that it was called solitude or pondering or anything. I just knew that I could think about things without as much interruption as I had in other settings.

A friend told of being out walking and having a distinct impression of being told that "I can't get through to you when you have those things in your ears." She immediately took out the ear buds, quit listening to whatever she had been listening to, and continued walking, this time receiving all kinds of good ideas.

The temple offers incredible opportunities for leaving the world outside and focusing on some of our deepest, sweetest thoughts. So many times when I go to the temple I wish I could have a holy little white computer in the celestial room to capture all the thoughts that come to me during this time of quiet, of stillness, of solitude. I find I can hardly wait to get home to write as much down as I can remember. It's like receiving sustenance! Spiritual nourishment. All the spiritual food groups are found in the temple and in other holy places.

There is time during sacrament meeting when we can focus on the Savior and our deep, personal thoughts. My own ward is large enough that we get quite a few minutes of solitude as the wonderful young men are helping us partake of the sacrament.

It may help us to focus on the words of the sacrament hymn we have sung—to ponder the meaning of the words. Or we may think of a favorite verse of scripture. Perhaps we think deeply about the covenants we are renewing.

As we take time for our personal prayers, I believe we can discover a "made-to-order" situation for being still, for asking questions and receiving impressions. I'm finding that as I listen more—not just for a longer time, but with more real intent—I receive more good ideas, more answers, more needed guidance.

I've discovered that I can find some solitude when I'm driving if I stay away from the fast lane and allow myself a little extra time to get where I'm going.

I really like the way Sister Patricia Holland spoke of such
things in a BYU Women's Conference talk several years ago:

> In dark and dangerous days, God will provide for us
> safe places, even wilderness places (I take that to mean
> sacred places undefiled by worldly civilization) where he
> protects us against evil and nourishes us with strength.
> Please allow yourself to take the time to go to that wil-
> derness retreat now, that sanctuary, if you will—the
> temple, your own home, places of privacy and revelation,
> places filled with prayer and meditation and scriptural
> truths. Allow yourselves to turn a few things down and
> turn a few things off. Seek to position yourselves prayer-
> fully in some solitude and serenity to receive the mind
> of God. Stop what you are so frantically doing and go
> into your private wilderness. Shut the door, turn out all
> earthly lights, set aside all earthly sights. Position your-
> self calmly, quietly in humble serenity until your prayer
> flows naturally, lovingly. When you feel God's presence,
> when you feel He is with you, you will be filled with a
> wonderful strength that will allow you to do anything
> in righteousness. Thus filled and strengthened, we can
> return to the battle, to some inevitable noise and com-
> motion and, yes, even some drudgery. But we do it more
> happily, more hopefully, more optimistically because we
> have communed with God and been filled with His joy,
> His charity, and His compassion, and we bear something
> of His light as we return. And because we are filled and
> strong, we can be a source of light, life, and love for oth-
> ers ("Filled with All the Fulness of God," 11).

May we not be too busy, too noisy, too distracted, too lonely, too preoccupied or too stubborn to seek for ways to be quiet, to discover the rewards and blessings of solitude, and to give way for the whisperings and influence of the Spirit in our souls.

Peace . . . PEACE . . . be still.

Chapter 8

And There Shall Come a Day

For he in whom we all believe
To us will all restore.
In patience, then, let us possess
Our souls till he appear.
"Sweet Is the Peace the Gospel Brings," *Hymns*, no. 14.

I used to spend quite a bit of time in a park called Memory Grove when I was a student nurse at the LDS Hospital in Salt Lake City. When we wanted to go to Temple Square or some other place in that area, we would hike down through Memory Grove. There was a little chapel there that had a very peaceful feeling in it. I loved just sitting there, thinking and feeling and reading a beautiful poem, "Immortality," by Frances Falk Miller, that was inscribed on the wall. The words of the poem were comforting to me when sad things happened, especially the idea that "there shall come a day" when all our difficulties will be made right.

I believe that there shall come a day when all our loneliness, our longing, our sorrow, will be turned to understanding and to joy.

There shall come a day when we will cry no more tears, when there will be no more death and no more loss.

There are so many scriptures and hymns and poems that speak of the comfort available to those who need it, and certainly that includes all who feel lonely. Although we may have to wait until the next life for everything to be sorted out completely, there is solace for the "here and now" in verses like these reminders of God's kindness and love:

"Verily I say unto you my friends, fear not, let your hearts be comforted; yea, rejoice evermore, and in everything give thanks;

"Waiting patiently on the Lord, for your prayers have entered into the ears of the Lord of Sabaoth, and are recorded with this seal and testament—the Lord hath sworn and decreed that they shall be granted.

"Therefore, he giveth this promise unto you, with an immutable covenant that they shall be fulfilled; and all things wherewith you have been afflicted shall work together for your good, and to my name's glory, saith the Lord" (Doctrine and Covenants 98:1–3).

"They shall hunger no more, neither thirst any more; neither shall the sun light on them, nor any heat.

"For the Lamb which is in the midst of the throne shall feed them, and shall lead them unto living fountains of waters: and God shall wipe away all tears from their eyes" (Revelation 7:16–17).

"God is our refuge and strength, a very present help in trouble" (Psalm 46:1).

"They that sow in tears shall reap in joy" (Psalm 126:5).

"Weeping may endure for a night, but joy cometh in the morning" (Psalm 30:5).

And read again some words, some phrases, from a few of our hymns—such tender, kind, gentle messages for those who need comfort. Don't just hurry through them. Think about them. Maybe you'll want to turn to some of the hymns and read all the verses.

"His love will find you and gently lead you From darkest night into day" ("Come unto Jesus," *Hymns,* no. 117).

"As thy days may demand, so thy succor shall be." ("How Firm a Foundation," *Hymns,* no. 85).

"Though outward ills await us here, The time, at longest, is not long" ("Though Deepening Trials," *Hymns,* no. 122).

"Dearest children, God is near you, Watching o'er you day and night" ("Dearest Children, God Is Near You," *Hymns,* no. 96).

"Cast thy burden upon the Lord, And he shall sustain thee" ("Cast Thy Burden upon the Lord," *Hymns,* no. 110).

"Let the Spirit heal our hearts Thru his quiet, gentle pow'r" ("Let the Holy Spirit Guide," *Hymns*, no. 143).

"Guide me as I search in weakness; Let thy loving light be mine" ("Lead Me into Life Eternal," *Hymns*, no. 45).

"The clouds ye so much dread Are big with mercy and shall break In blessings on your head" ("God Moves in a Mysterious Way," *Hymns*, no. 285).

In the hymn "Lead, Kindly Light" (*Hymns*, no. 97), there is a phrase that's been on my mind a lot as I've worked on this book: "The night is dark, and I am far from home . . ."

Dear friends, maybe that's what we're feeling so much of the time when loneliness is all around us. We are far from HOME—from our heavenly Home, and from our heavenly parents kind and dear.

May we feel their love for us, their tender watchcare, even when we're alone.

None of us will be forced to look to the Savior for answers to the hunger in our soul, but I'm convinced He really is the Way, the only Way, that we ultimately have our tears dried, our hearts healed, our loneliness assuaged, and our hopes and dreams fulfilled.

Alma, in giving counsel to his son Helaman, helps him understand the importance of putting his trust in God: "For I do know that whosoever shall put their trust in God shall be supported in their trials, and their troubles, and their afflictions, and shall be lifted up at the last day" (Alma 36:3).

I notice that we will be *supported in* our trials, troubles, and afflictions (including loneliness), rather than being *removed from* them.

Elder Orson F. Whitney wrote: "No pain that we suffer, no trial that we experience is wasted. It ministers to our education, to the development of such qualities as patience, faith, fortitude and humility. All that we suffer and all that we endure, especially when we endure it patiently, builds up our characters, purifies our hearts, expands our souls, and makes us more tender and charitable, more worthy to be called the children of God . . . and it is through sorrow and suffering, toil and tribulation, that we gain the education that we come here to acquire and which will make us more like our Father and Mother in heaven" (cited by Spencer W. Kimball in *Faith Precedes the Miracle*, 98).

I've already included some phrases from several hymns that I find incredibly comforting, but I've chosen one that I want to share in its entirety:

> *Come, ye disconsolate, where'er ye languish;*
> *Come to the mercy seat, fervently kneel.*
> *Here bring your wounded hearts; here tell your anguish.*
> *Earth has no sorrow that heav'n cannot heal.*
>
> *Joy of the desolate, Light of the straying,*
> *Hope of the penitent, fadeless and pure!*
> *Here speaks the Comforter, tenderly saying,*
> *"Earth has no sorrow that heav'n cannot cure."*
>
> *Here see the Bread of Life; see waters flowing*
> *Forth from the throne of God, pure from above.*

Come to the feast of love; come, ever knowing
Earth has no sorrow but heav'n can remove.
("Come, Ye Disconsolate," Hymns, no. 115)

Oh, I *know* this is true. These words bring tears to my eyes. I feel deeply that someday our loneliness will be swept away.

There is *no* sorrow, including loneliness, that heaven cannot heal, cure, and remove! Please know that. Please *feel* that as you go through your deep water and fiery trials, through all the times when you feel alone. *Know* that you are never completely alone.

Bring your wounded hearts. Tell your anguish.

Come to the mercy seat. Come to the feast of love!

One reason I love this hymn is because it helps me express some of my feelings about being alone, and about loneliness, and about the trials and burdens that are part of our lives.

When people ask me, "How come you're always happy?" I usually give a short answer, something like, "Because I've tried being unhappy, and I like being happy better." But my real answer is that I trust God. It may be a short answer, but it comes from the center of my soul.

I DO trust God. I know that I am His child. I know that He loves me and even likes me, and I feel Him cry with me. And sometimes I feel Him smile and even laugh with me. I can count on Him. He will never leave me alone or comfortless.

You have read some of my stories, have become acquainted with some of my experiences, and I hope you have noticed the fact—the sweet reality—that He has always, *always* been very close. He hasn't stopped everything difficult from happening, but He has let me know I'm not struggling alone. He has allowed me to learn some extraordinary lessons, and I can feel Him smile when He knows I "get it."

My trust in Him includes the conviction that He does *nothing* to try to punish me or hurt me. Every single thing He has asked of me has been for my ultimate good. I strongly, deeply believe that. It doesn't mean I haven't had some extremely difficult experiences in my life, but I do know that "earth has no sorrow that heav'n cannot heal"!

I know that loneliness is prevalent, and that there are many who seem to feel a sense of being alone, of being lonely, almost constantly. I'm so sorry about it, but I know that it does not have to be terminal. I have prayed that we will never forget what the Savior has promised. May we take this very personally, and may it bring sweet comfort and assurance.

"Be patient in afflictions, for thou shalt have many; but endure them, for, lo, I am with thee, even unto the end of thy days" (Doctrine and Covenants 24:8).

"I am he; yea, I am he that comforteth you" (2 Nephi 8:12).

"I will not leave you comfortless: I will come to you" (John 14:18).

"I will never leave thee, nor forsake thee" (Hebrews 13:5).

"Wherefore, be of good cheer, and do not fear, for I the Lord am with you, and will stand by you" (Doctrine and Covenants 68:6).

And there shall come a day when He will wrap His loving arms around us.

And there shall come a day when we will rest from all care and all sorrow.

And there shall come a day when sweet reunions will bring us back to our dear ones.

And there shall come a day when we will have no more tears of sorrow, only tears of joy.

I am confident that day will come.

So buck up, little buckaroo, little child of God. He loves you dearly and is watching over you always. Come unto Him, and your soul will hunger no more.

"And God shall wipe away all tears from their eyes; and there shall be no more death, neither sorrow, nor crying, neither shall there be any more pain" (Revelation 21:4).

Sources

Bell, Elouise. "Peace, Be Still." In *Women Steadfast in Christ*. Salt Lake City: Deseret Book, 1992, 19–31.

Benson, Ezra Taft. *God, Family, Country: Our Three Great Loyalties*. Salt Lake City: Deseret Book, 1974.

Frank, Anne, Otto Frank, and Mirjam Pressler. *The Diary of a Young Girl*. New York: Doubleday, 1995.

Hales, Robert D. "The Aaronic Priesthood: Return with Honor." *Ensign*, May 1990.

Hill, John Wesley. *Abraham Lincoln—Man of God*. New York: G. P. Putnam's Sons, 1927.

Hinckley, Gordon B. *Teachings of Gordon B. Hinckley*. Salt Lake City: Deseret Book, 1997.

———. "This Is the Work of the Master." *Ensign*, May 1995.

———. "Women of the Church." *Ensign*, November 1996.

Holland, Jeffrey R. "None Were with Him." *Ensign*, May 2009.

———. "This Do in Remembrance of Me," *Ensign*, November 1995.

Holland, Patricia T. "Filled with All the Fulness of God." In *Clothed with Charity: Talks from the 1996 Women's Conference*, 1–12.

Sources

Hymns of The Church of Jesus Christ of Latter-day Saints. Salt Lake City: The Church of Jesus Christ of Latter-day Saints, 1985.

Journal of Discourses. 26 vols. London: Latter-day Saints' Book Depot, 1853–1886.

Keller, Helen. *The Story of My Life.* New York: Doubleday, Page and Company, 1905.

Kimball, Spencer W. *Faith Precedes the Miracle.* Salt Lake City: Deseret Book, 1972.

Lee, Harold B. *Decisions for Successful Living.* Salt Lake City: Deseret Book, 1973.

MacDonald, Joan B. *The Holiness of Everyday Life.* Salt Lake City: Deseret Book, 1995.

Maxwell, Neal A. *Of One Heart.* Salt Lake City: Deseret Book, 1975.

———. *We Will Prove Them Herewith.* Salt Lake City: Deseret Book, 1982.

———. *Wherefore, Ye Must Press Forward.* Salt Lake City: Deseret Book, 1977.

Mother Teresa of Calcutta. *A Gift for God, Prayers and Meditations.* New York: Harper and Row, 1975.

O'Grady, Scott, with Jeff Coplon. *Return with Honor.* New York: Doubleday, 1995.

Smith, Joseph. *History of The Church of Jesus Christ of Latterday Saints.* 7 vols. Salt Lake City: The Church of Jesus Christ of Latter-day Saints, 1932–1951.

———. *Teachings of the Prophet Joseph Smith.* Joseph Fielding Smith, ed. and comp. Salt Lake City: Deseret Book, 1976.

Thayne, Emma Lou. "Learning Is Nurture." In *Women of Wisdom and Knowledge: Talks Selected from the BYU Women's Conferences.* Salt Lake City: Deseret Book, 1990, 99–106.

Tolstoy, Leo. *What Men Live By.* N.p., 1881.

Whitney, Orson F. *Life of Heber C. Kimball.* Salt Lake City: n.p., 1888.

Wirthlin, Joseph B. "Valued Companions." *Ensign,* November 1997.

About the Author

Mary Ellen Edmunds has served as director of training at the Missionary Training Center in Provo, Utah, and as a member of the Relief Society general board. She graduated from the College of Nursing at Brigham Young University, has been a faculty member at BYU, and has served full-time missions in Asia and Africa. A favorite speaker and author, Mary Ellen has published many books and talks, including *The Mary Ellen Edmunds Collection* and *You Can Never Get Enough of What You Don't Need.*